Politically Correct Guns

D0096049

Other books by Alan Gottlieb
The Gun Grabbers
Alan Gottlieb's Celebrity Address Book
Gun Rights Fact Book
The Rights of Gun Owners
The Gun Owner's Political Action Manual

With George Flynn:
Guns for Women

With Ron Arnold:
Trashing the Economy
Politically Correct Environment

With David Kopel
Things You Can Do
To Defend Your Gun Rights
More Things You Can Do
To Defend Your Gun Rights

Edited:
The Wise Use Agenda
Fear of Food

Politically Correct Guns

Alan Gottlieb

MERRIL PRESS
BELLEVUE, WASHINGTON

First Edition
Published by Merril Press

Merril Press, a division of Merril Mail Marketing, Inc.,
is an independent publisher and distributor of books
to the trade, P.O. Box 1682, Bellevue, Washington
98009. Telephone 206-454-7009. Fax 206-451-3959.
Additional copies of this quality paperback book
may be ordered from Merril Press at $14.95 each.
E-mail: Internet: 74123.3036@compuserve.com.

Organizations and grass roots groups interested in using this book in their public education or fund-raising
projects may contact Merril Press for quantity discounts.

Typeset in Bookman Old Style, on AMSi computers by
Merril Press, Bellevue, Washington. Cover design by
Northwoods Studio. Selected graphics by Corel.

LIBRARY OF CONGRESS CATALOGING-IN-PUBLICATION DATA

Gottlieb, Alan M.
    Politically correct guns / Alan Gottlieb.
        p.   cm.
    ISBN   0-936783-16-8 (pbk.)
    1. Gun control—Humor. 2. Firearms—Humor. I. Title.
PN6231.G95G67   1996
363.4'5'0973—dc20   96-1533
                                                    CIP

PRINTED IN THE UNITED STATES OF AMERICA

Table of Contents

Part Three:
How to Shoot Yourself in the Foot
Page 113

Acknowledgments

After all the serious books I've written on the rights of gun owners, it's time to take a humor break. There's enough silliness in the gun control crowd to keep us laughing for years. So here's my effort to bring a smile and a belly-laugh to a sometimes heavy debate.

Politically Correct Guns is chock full of anti-gun nuts and salt-of-the-earth gun owners defending their rights—so you might say it's full of salted nuts. I've spoofed all kinds of Gun Grabbers in these pages, and I had the kind of help putting this book together that has always come from dedicated gun rights advocates.

First, let me thank my editor Ron Arnold for keeping my drafts on schedule and providing helpful suggestions along the way. And Ken Jacobson, Executive Director of the Citizens Committee for the Right to Keep and Bear Arms, helped not only with excellent ideas but also called upon his talents as an art director to produce those great drawings of anti-gun shootist Carl "Rambo" Rowan you'll see later.

Chuck Asay kindly gave permission to use his outstanding pro-gun political cartoons. Many thanks to Corel Corporation for permission to use their wonderful Gallery illustrations that liven up our pages. And thanks to Northwoods Studio for the snappy book cover.

Most of all, thanks to my wife Julianne and my children Amy, Merril, Alexis and Andrew for keeping my sense of humor sharpened.

Dedication

To all those gun owners
whose support has made
my work possible

FOREWORD

To: Alan Gottlieb
From: Bill Clinton

You know, Alan, I've been meaning to write this note to you for some time.

First, let me just say that I'm not such a bad guy when it comes to guns. Why, I always like to say that some of my best friends are gun owners. You ought to write a book about some of them one day: like Sen. Teddy Kennedy's bodyguard and West Virginia's Sen. John D. Rockefeller, IV.

What's more, I don't feel that we should be enemies. I know you may find it hard to believe, but I'm really not a gun grabber. I want to explain to you the real reason why I pushed for, and signed into law, all those anti-gun bills—because after I explain it to you, I know we can be friends.

The first one was the Brady Law. Now that was a matter of self defense. If Hillary caught me one more time with a girlfriend and there wasn't a waiting period, well, you understand. Don't you?

What about the ban on assault weapons and high capacity magazines? Believe me, Alan, it was pure and simple economics. I'll bet you're wondering why I took so long to sign it into law

xi

after Congress passed it. Well, I needed time to go from gun show to gun show and buy up scores of those assault rifles and high capacity magazines. When I sell them in the years to come, it's going to make the profits on that cattle future deal look like Jimmy Carter's peanuts. I really sucker punched the anti-gunners by creating the hysteria that fueled gun sales to an all-time record level and made big profits for your industry friends.

You see? I'm your friend. I pledge to you that after you help me win a second term, I'll give you a real good deal on some assault rifles.

And you know I'm an avid hunter. Some have criticized me for not keeping a good hunting dog in the White House, but you don't know what a great hunting cat we have here in Socks. Tell them what a great bird cat you are, Socks.

FIRST FELINE: MEOW, MEOW, MEOW.

Thank you, Socks. And if you want a place to hunt, I've still got some of that land back in Arkansas. We didn't sell many lots, so you can hunt on it if you like. It's called Whitewater.

And Alan, keep up the good work, but please stop attacking me on all those doggone radio and TV shows, okay? Thank you.

Your friend Bill.

No, it's not really from the President, but here's the book he didn't say I should write.

Alan Gottlieb
Liberty Park
Bellevue, Washington

Politically Correct Guns

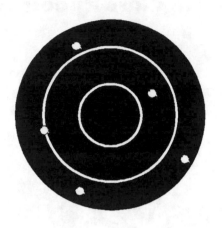

Part One

Tales of Hypocrisy

Alan's Dictionary: **hy•poc•ri•sy** *n* 1 : the act or practice of pretending to be what one is not or to have principles or beliefs that one does not have, *for example:* a gun control nut who owns a gun or hires an armed bodyguard.

Don't attempt to adjust the controls on your TV. I'm about to take you to a place so strange even the Twilight Zone can't handle it: the American anti-gun scene! So, here, ladies and gentlemen, we begin our journey through the crazy world of gun grabbers and politics. You'll soon realize we've entered—(weird theme music)—the Hypocrisy Zone....

World Class Hypocrites

Case #1

Teddy and the Bodyguard

Nowhere in the pages of history can one find a grosser champion of gun control than Senator Edward Moore Kennedy of Massachusetts. The Hero of Chappaquiddick has attacked the Second Amendment so many times that nowadays the old document nervously reaches for its holster every time it sees him coming.

Ted Kennedy shoots back. This politico who has sponsored one anti-gun bill after another for many years seems to think guns are just fine if they're defending *his* life. Guns are only bad if they're defending *yours*.

The crowning achievement of Teddy Kennedy's speckled career came in January, 1986, when the Senator hired one Charles A. Stein, Jr., a private bodyguard, to protect him on a junket to

South America. Stein, a former California police officer who had worked for Kennedy for several years, came to the Capitol just hours before "wheels up" time at the airport to make final departure arrangements with his client.

Chuck Stein parked his car on Capitol Hill—Washington, D.C. has some of the strictest anti-gun laws in the nation—and walked in at the Russell Senate Office Building.

Now visualize this next scene with Sylvester Stallone playing Chuck Stein in *Teddy's Bodyguard—The Movie*: At the front desk, Stein/Stallone says, "Yo, guard! Hey, I wanna check my heat wit' youse guys while I go up to Teddy's office."

Out of Stein/Stallone's travel bag come two submachine guns, a pistol and 146 rounds of ammunition.

The U.S. Capitol police looked at this arsenal and promptly busted Stein, who was
hauled off to jail and charged with three counts
of D.C. anti-gun law violations. The guns were
impounded.

Teddy went ballistic.

"How can a gun law be so stupid?" he
shouted at a mirror on the wall. "I'm a very important man. I need my armed bodyguard!"

Stein, a retired captain of the San
Fernando Police Department, was licensed to
carry firearms in California and was authorized
by the State Department to use the guns in foreign countries, but had no license to carry firearms in Washington, D.C.   The District of
Columbia's anti-gun laws prohibit the possession
of handguns not registered in the city prior to
February 5, 1977, and they outlaw the possession
of automatic firearms.

Yes, it's a stupid law, and Kennedy's bodyguard got caught trying to surrender the weapons
to what he thought was the proper authority. But
he tried to check his guns with the U.S. Capitol
Police, not the Washington, D.C. Police Department. If he had surrendered the guns to a D.C.
officer, he would have been granted immunity from
prosecution. But he didn't, and he thereby broke
the law.

Did Teddy the Gun Grabber respect the law
of Washington, D.C.? Not on his sweet life.

He called U.S. Attorney General Edwin
Meese III to have his bodyguard released and his
guns returned. Kennedy's staff also contacted D.C.
Police Chief Maurice Turner to protest the injus-
tice.

Stein was released on his own recognizance, but the guns to defend Teddy were held as evidence to be destroyed when the case was closed.

When the *Washington Post* called to ask about Kennedy's disregard of D.C.'s gun law, Bob Mann, Teddy's spokesman, told them that the bodyguard "assumed he was doing the appropriate thing rather than leave them unattended in an automobile, but because of this technical glitch in the law, he was stopped."

This technical glitch? Glitch?

An absolute prohibition against possessing automatic weapons is a technical glitch? An absolute prohibition against possessing handguns is a technical glitch?

If you're Ready Teddy, the law is just a technical glitch—when it inconveniences you. When it flattens some little guy trying to defend his own life from criminals, it's a good sound law for all the people.

> # Ted Kennedy's car has killed more people than my gun

Reminder to the Hero of Chappaquiddick

Ask the Virginia real estate manager who used a gun to hold an escaped mental patient and two drug pushers he found in his D.C. rental property—and got arrested for it. Ted Kennedy didn't call the U.S. Attorney General to get that guy out of jail.

As things turned out, Teddy and two sisters, Jean Smith and Pat Lawford, left as scheduled in the late afternoon of January 7 for a 12-day trip to Brazil, Argentina, Peru and Uruguay.

Before Kennedy departed, Treasury Secretary James A. Baker III authorized Secret Service protection for the first few days of the trip.

Stein was out of jail in time to join Teddy in mid-trip, and was provided firearms by the U.S. embassies in each of the countries Kennedy visited. The guns were returned to the embassies upon Kennedy's departure.

They were evidently much in need. *U.S. News and World Report* filed a story indicating that Kennedy was not a hit in South America, especially not in Chile. Teddy's motorcade there was greeted with a street salad of eggs, tomatoes and rocks as he visited the Chilean capital January 15. The protest was ostensibly against the human rights record of Augusto Pinochet. Kennedy's car was struck and a Chilean rights leader was injured by demonstrators backing the junta.

Teddy stuck his tongue out at the nation by pointedly noting that his stand on gun control had not changed a bit because of the embarrassing incident. He has continued to introduce one rigid anti-gun bill after another in every new session of Congress.

But that wasn't the end of it for Stein. He went back to California and his security firm. However, the charges against him stood back in D.C. He went to the D.C. Court of Appeals asking them to dismiss the weapons charges. A divided panel refused to dismiss them.

As if to show how stupid the law is, Judge John A. Terry wrote in his majority opinion that a person can be immune from prosecution in the District if he voluntarily turns over his gun to a D.C. police officer. But he said the protection did not apply to Stein, who tried to leave his guns for a short time with the U.S. Capitol Police, which is not affiliated with the city's police department.

Judge Julia Cooper Mack wrote in her sharply worded dissent that the distinction between the D.C. police and U.S. Capitol Police was a "hypertechnical statutory interpretation" that generated an "absurd and harsh result."

"In fact, prosecuting Stein for choosing the wrong police officer to surrender his weapons to only works to discourage other citizens from being so forthcoming in the future," Mack wrote.

The District's ridiculously strict anti-gun statute has generated tremendous controversy among out-of-towners. Private investigators and bodyguards are frequently arrested for carrying a weapon that they are licensed elsewhere to have. Most arrests happen at the Capitol, which daily has thousands of out-of-state visitors, including security personnel. The Capitol Police, with their metal detectors at every door, catch legitimate gun-toting bodyguards with annoying frequency. Even out-of-state police officers in town for extradition hearings are breaking the law if they take their guns and are not licensed in the District.

Frequent non-licensed gun arrests are such a problem in the nation's capital that Senator Ted Stevens (R-Alaska) has urged reform in the District's gun laws. Everybody in Alaska carries a gun, Senator Stevens notes, and people sometimes have forgotten to leave them at home when they visit Stevens' office in the Senate.

Senator Ted Stevens is a long-time defender of the rights of gun owners and has little patience with the nonsense of D.C's anti-gun laws. If it was up to him, legitimate licensed gun owners would be treated in their nation's capital like they are at home.

Whatever became of Chuck Stein? Well, according to his attorney Stephen Braga, the appeal was rebuffed and the trial court reduced his six felony counts of weapons violations on a plea to one misdemeanor count, for which Stein paid a $1,000 fine. Stein took a "tough" fall! But Teddy the Gun Grabber, unscathed, marches on to the same old tune of gun control.

Losing Touch

This *Chicago Tribune* political cartoon apparently expressed the mood of the country that brought down a decades-long congressional dominance by the Democratic Party.

President Clinton's noisy appeal to the fears of voters certainly backfired in the elections of 1994.

The three issues chosen by the cartoonist to needle Clinton are indicative of public concerns that mattered at the polls: An activist Congress, the Social Security program and gun control.

If the outcome at the polls was any indication, people were tired of all three sacred cows and wanted to see some changes.

It's fascinating that stick-in-the-mud gun control advocates like Teddy Kennedy don't want to listen.

A Question of I.Q.

I might be missing something, but I thought criminals were the ones that ought to be controlled. Politicians keep trying to control guns instead. While nobody has given a gun an I.Q. test, it seems reasonable to say that a gun doesn't have the intelligence to pull its own trigger.

"They decided to turn me loose and lynch my pistol."

Distinguished political cartoonist Bill Mauldin draws on the same subject. His 1982 cartoon catches the central hypocrisy of the gun control crowd. It's all just ideology that lets the crook go and lynches the pistol. During the O. J. Simpson trial we didn't see any mad rush to crank up a knife control movement.

THE MINUTE MAN BY DANIEL CHESTER FRENCH

MODIFIED BY THE ANTI-GUN NUTS

History as it are rewrote

Thumbnail Horror Story #1

Philip Russell Coleman worked late at a Louisiana liquor store. He felt he needed a handgun to protect himself. His application to purchase a chrome-plated .380 caliber Lorcin pistol was approved three days after Coleman was shot to death in a mid-1995 holdup. He'd never been convicted of a felony, or had a past history of drug abuse or mental illness. Another citizen killed by the Brady law's waiting period. He was 42.

If you support Gun Control, put
this yard sign in front of your home.
If not, join us in our fight to preserve
your right to keep and bear arms.

Citizens Committee for the Right to Keep and Bear Arms
Annual Membership $15 / 12500 N.E. 10th Pl., Bellevue, WA 98005 / (206) 454-4911

'The way to stop this madness
is by outlawing rocks'

Famous political cartoonist Bill Mauldin drew
many biting parodies of the Gun Grabber mental-
ity for the *Chicago Sun-Times* during the late
1970s and early 1980s. Even though the specific
issues he satirized are of only historical interest
today, his basic message remains as fresh as the

'None of this stuff works, but it sure sells'

day he drew them: Gun control doesn't work—can't work—because it is a wrongheaded approach to the problem of criminality. Mauldin is of special historical interest because he occasionally turned his incisive pen to the gun lobby and roasted them with the same wit as he did the anti-gun lobby.

World Class Hypocrites

Case #2

Jay Rockefeller's Colt AR-15

In late 1994, Congress approved a crime bill carrying provisions that banned so-called assault-style weapons. After the bill was signed into law by President Clinton, no new purchases of such guns could be made.

The *New York Times* commented on the crime bill by racheting up their gun control demands. "Keep on Pushing Gun Control," their editorial page snarled. "Americans still live in a dangerous society armed with tens of millions of largely unregistered weapons."

Tougher gun controls are now possible after winning the battle over banning semiautomatic weapons, chirped the *Times*, given "the healthier public attitude toward weapons that have no purpose other than the shooting of people."

The Colt AR-15 semiautomatic rifle is just such a weapon. It has no other purpose than the shooting of people, so the *Times* and other critics claimed.

Now, are you ready for this?

One of the men voting for the ban, West Virginia Senator John D. Rockefeller IV, known simply as "Jay," happens to own one himself.

Yes, the scion of the Standard Oil Trust family owned a Colt AR-15 semiautomatic rifle at the very moment he voted to stop you and me from buying one. The law was not retroactive, so he didn't have to give up his AR-15. You just can't have yours, that's all.

It gets worse.

In an August 23, 1994, edition of the *Charleston Daily Mail*, Sen. Rockefeller told the paper's Washington bureau that a friend of his had given him the AR-15 25 years ago. So the paper wrote this interesting paragraph:

"Rockefeller keeps the rifle—'a terrific weapon'—in his Washington home."

That report attracted the attention of the *Washington Times'* "Inside the Beltway" columnist, John McCaslin, who quoted District police officials as saying possession of an AR-15 in the District without the permission of law-enforcement officials happens to be a felony. District officials had no record of semiautomatic weapons registered under Sen. Rockefeller's name.

That's an odd oversight for someone with the savvy and resources of Jay Rockefeller, who served as Governor of West Virginia from 1977.

Just think of it! Jay
Rockefeller as a convicted
felon! Can't you visualize
Senator Rockefeller debating a
fine point of the law on the Senate
floor in his convict's uniform?
The President *Pro Tempore* of the
Senate recognizes the gentleman
from West Virginia, who is un-
handcuffed to make his point.
"Oh, how stunning! The
stripes, the black and white,
Jay—it's ever so *you!* It's *très chic,*   dahling.
Er... Uh... Ahem, the floor is yours, Senator
Rockefeller."

McCaslin's column stirred things up in the
senator's office. They fell all over themselves
asserting that, as a matter of fact, Senator
Rockefeller had never actually kept the weapon
in his fashionable D.C. home off Rock Creek
Parkway.

For the past four years it had been stored
in Northern Virginia by the Senator's personal
security detail. Prior to that, the Senator had
kept it in West Virginia, where possession of AR-
15s is not against the law.

Now, why would Senator Rockefeller want
to own a Colt AR-15, a gun whose only purpose,
say critics, is to shoot people?

Could it be for personal protection? Well,
probably not. Jay Rockefeller enjoys a level of
private security unknown to most Americans and
round-the-clock protection on Capitol Hill by
police. He could hardly say he needed it for self-
defense.

A Rockefeller spokesperson, Laura Quinn, told the *Washington Times* that though he had briefly used it for some target shooting a long time ago, he was just a "collector" now.

But you and I can't be collectors, thanks in part, to Jay Rockefeller.

However, Ms. Quinn consoled, if any of the Senator's constituents are interested in getting an AR-15, they can't do that, but they can go out and maybe get some of the other assault-style weapons left untouched by the ban.

And every voter in West Virginia should know that they can count on the Senator to oppose any legislation requiring them to surrender their weapons. That would affect him, too, and Jay Rockefeller is not about to give up his guns. *No, Sireee! From my cold dead fingers! Make my day! Us Rockefellers is just good ol' boys.*

The editorial page of the *Washington Times* had this to say:

"If the senator appears to be in an awkward position here, it's because he is. It's bad enough to sign off on legislation banning law-abiding citizens access to weapons they may want to 'collect.' Even more difficult is trying to explain why the senator's constituents should not be allowed to obtain a weapon that he himself enjoys. Why is he to be trusted with one any more than they are?"

Hmm, good question.

When guns are outlawed,
only Rockefellers
will have guns.

HELLO, MRS. JONES? YOUR FIVE-DAY WAITING PERIOD IS OVER NOW! YOU CAN COME IN AND PICK UP YOUR .38 ANYTIME! HELLO? MRS. JONES... ARE YOU THERE?

Famous cartoon commentary by
Chuck Asay on the Brady Law

Thumbnail Horror Story #2

April, 1995: When Domino's Pizza deliveryman Anthony Leone reached for the .45-caliber he keeps on his car seat, he thought he was foiling a robbery attempt by a couple who had hit him in the face. Did Domino's give him a medal?

No, they fired him. Domino's officials said he was violating company policy that prohibits drivers from carrying weapons. Leone, 34, a marksman in training for U.S. Olympics competition and who competed for the Army Reserve and National Guard, worked for 2½ years at a Domino's in Woodbridge, Virginia, near Washington, D.C. The job gave him the flexibility to go to school at Northern Virginia Community College and compete as a rifle marksman. No good deed will go unpunished.

TANK McNAMARA

One of many comic strips on gun control

The Wizard of Id weighs in on gun control

Practically every syndicated comic strip in the
United States has one way or another touched
upon the question of gun control and gun rights.
The Wizard of Id did its usual inimitable magic.
Well, what can you say after a punch line like that?

World Class Hypocrites

Case #3

Anti-gun Advocate
Jennifer O'Neill

How many times have you heard this story: "I was cleaning my gun when it went off."

Usually it's an old high school rival or a business competitor or a soured spouse that gets in the way of the stray bullet.

Not in the case of the sultry movie actress Jennifer O'Neill, best known for her portrayal of the older woman to the teenage Gary Grimes in the movie *Summer of '42*. In a 1982 incident, she shot *herself*. In the abdomen. Here's the bite:

Jennifer O'Neill is a gun control advocate. Big time. Ban the gun, ban the bullet, ban imports, exports, toys, the whole shot. But she kept the gun for personal protection.

If you like heaping hot hypocrisy, you'll love this one.

The screen beauty, who was 33 at the time, shot herself while cleaning her .38-caliber revolver in the bedroom of her colonial-style mansion. Her home was located on a sprawling 22-acre estate on McLain Street in exclusive Bedford Hills, New York. The place was guarded by a heavy metal gate and eight German shepherd attack dogs trained to go for assailants holding a gun. Her manager-husband John Lederer was at home at the time, along with the housekeeper and O'Neill's year-old son, Reis.

The seductive actress was wearing a pair of jeans and a sweater when she shot herself as she lay on her bed in a second-floor bedroom at 6 p.m. on Friday evening, October 22, 1982.

She was able to dial the operator, who then routed the emergency call to the police.

Police quoted O'Neill as gasping on the line, "Please help me. My God. The gun went off."

Lt. Theodore Brugger, who took the call, said, "She was talking very slowly. She was obviously in a tremendous amount of pain."

Husband John Lederer was not aware that anything had happened until he saw the police cars.

Bedford Hills Police Chief David Marden told reporters the shooting was "purely accidental."

"She was cleaning her gun when it went off," he said noncommittally.

Police on the day of the shooting said they had not yet been able to talk to the actress, who was taken to Northern Westchester Hospital in Mount Kisco, to clear up lingering mysteries about the accident.

Authorities said the bullet appeared to have entered her abdomen, passed through her body and exited through her back. She underwent surgery at 6:36 p.m. and remained in the hospital's intensive care unit for a short time. She was then listed in fair condition and began her slow recovery.

Detective Sergeant Thomas Rothwell told reporters he hoped to question her at the hospital. Miss O'Neill's lawyer was scheduled to be present.

Police at first declined to say whether her revolver was registered. But they said no charges were going to be filed against her.

However, they changed their minds within a few days and charged O'Neill with a misdemeanor weapons count and her husband was charged with criminal possession of a weapon, a felony.

O'Neill faced up to a year in jail if convicted. Lederer, who was 34 at the time, could have been sentenced to as much as seven years in prison if convicted. Snared by New York's tough anti-gun laws that Jennifer O'Neill helped pass with her advocacy of gun control laws and support of anti-gun groups.

Her lawyer, Lawrence Maffel, took the case   and   in   due   time   argued   before Westchester County Judge Carmine Marasco that the actress, as a celebrity, had a right to carry a gun to protect herself and her family. A strange argument in defense of a noisy anti-gun advocate, hmm?

Maffel told the Westchester court that his client kept the unlicensed .38 revolver in the house because she had received anti-Semitic death threats and hate mail.

Maffel also said that O'Neill had been considered for a television series but that the studio would not sign her to a contract while the case was in progress. Poor baby.

In the pretrial motion Maffel disclosed the threats which he said forced O'Neill "to install, at great expense, an elaborate security system at her home."

Maffel declared, "As with all public figures, a certain amount of mail or calls from the lunatic fringe is to be expected. However, Miss O'Neill has been repeatedly subjected to hate mail and death threats."

He claimed one of the threats was from a self-styled American Nazi who made threats against Ms. O'Neill's husband because he is Jewish.

While the case made its way through the courts, Jennifer O'Neill went on ABC Television's "Good Morning America" program on December 2, and explained her version of the incident.

She said she saw the gun in an open bedroom safe. Fearing that her young son Reis, "could come in and reach it, I took the gun out

of the safe and put it
on the bed.

"I was trying
to   ascertain
whether   it   was
loaded, because I
wanted to get it
away, and it went
off."

Miss O'Neill
did not explain why
she   and   Lederer
wanted the gun in addition to their elaborate
home security system. She also did not dis-
cuss why she hadn't applied for a pistol license.
There is nothing in New York law to prevent
actresses and other celebrities from applying
for pistol licenses like everyone else.

On February 26, 1983, The *New York
Times* reported that Judge Marasco had ruled
that O'Neill must stand trial on the charge of
illegal possession of a weapon.

The case finally went to trial in early January of 1984 in a White Plains, New York, court.
The prosecution tried to prove that the gun belonged to Lederer and O'Neill. The gun involved
in the accidental shooting was brought into the
courtroom during the trial for O'Neill to identify.

Miss O'Neill said she didn't really know
much about handguns and couldn't be sure if
that was the one with which she shot herself.

Both Jennifer O'Neill and John Lederer
told the judge that they didn't know how the gun
got there in the house.

Whoa! Two intelligent people are telling

the equally intelligent judge they didn't know how that gun got in their house?

Yep. They pulled off the old "Duh, what?" defense.

The prosecution couldn't prove them wrong. They couldn't prove who the weapon belonged to because it was not registered as required by New York law.

The judge dismissed charges against both Lederer and O'Neill on January 10, 1984. Had Lederer been convicted, he would have faced a mandatory jail term of up to seven years because of a previous conviction.

Case closed.

You can argue that the gun law in New York is absurdly strict, which it is. You can argue that Jennifer O'Neill indeed had the right to defend her life and property with a handgun, which she had—all she lacked was the license.

But you can't argue that a dedicated anti-gun advocate and supporter of anti-gun groups isn't hypocritical for having a gun in her house with which to shoot herself in the belly—even if the prosecutor couldn't prove who owned the gun.

Gee, judge, I don't know how that gun got in my house, if that's the gun.

I must admit that I'm impressed with the nerve it took to say that. My grade-school son wouldn't believe that one. I never cease to wonder at the sheer brass of the anti-gun crowd. What a bunch!

Well, that's the Gun Grabbers for you.

This political cartoon is the kind of anti-gun stuff Jennifer O'Neill supported. It tells us that if you're a gun owner, you must be a crook.

World Class Hypocrites

Case #4

New York City

How can a city be a hypocrite?
Read on, read on....
Return with me now to those thrilling days of yesteryear, to 1974, when John V. Lindsay was mayor of New York City.

He has just received the survey that he ordered a year earlier. It was to determine how many city employees were authorized to carry firearms.

Not counting police, Lindsay finds that one out of every forty of his city employees had permits to carry weapons. That amounted to more than 9,000 city employees who weren't cops running around with guns. Lindsay ran on a strict gun control platform. He was embarrassed.

The survey, conducted by Investigation
Commissioner Nicholas Scoppetta, discovered
that letters of authorization for gun permits were
being written for numerous underlings without
the knowledge of their  superiors and
that a large
number of gun
licenses had
been issued
by the Police
Department
without the
benefit of
any letter of
authorization.

Here's the nub of this nugget:
One of those with a permit to carry was
one Sidney Baumgarten, who had been assistant in charge of gun control to Mayor Abe Beam,
who served before Lindsay won the spot.
Hmm....
New York City has become infamous for its
ridiculously stringent—and unevenly applied—
anti-gun laws. Accusations of preferential treatment for a wide array of prominent politicians and
other public figures have been a major feature in
New York City headlines for decades, and the cops
always covered for the officials who were dishing
out the licenses to the elite.
For example, in 1976, things were so bad
that the Federation of Greater New York Rifle and
Pistol Clubs asked Police Commissioner Michael
J. Codd to open approved pistol license records
to public inspection.

In making their case, the Federation cited 18 names of people about whom they had "specific information that each of the named persons are indeed licensed, or have been licensed, to carry pistols by the New York Police Department. The list contained the names of sanitation union chief John DeLury and the anti-gun *New York Times* publisher Arthur Ochs "Punch" Sulzberger.

New York City gun laws are so strict that applicants must show a "need or special danger" and endure an investigation by the Pistol License Bureau. New York State penal law contains a provision that the "application for any license, if granted, shall be a public record." However, the Police Department steadfastly refused to provide access to the gun records.

That's not nice.

The Federation was out to prove that some prominent individuals got their licenses in a much shorter period than the average person, showing favoritism and elitism. In addition to the union boss and *New York Times* publisher, gun permits were unofficially confirmed for Dr. Milton Brothers, husband of celebrity psychologist Dr. Joyce Brothers; Dr. Frank Field, science reporter and weatherman for WNBC-TV; Rep. James Scheuer, Democrat from Queens; Rocky Aoki, owner of the Benihana Japanese restaurants; and a dozen others. The best known name of the Federation's list was that of former Mayor John V. Lindsay, who did not have a pistol license. With his stand on gun control, it would have been political suicide for him to get a license, said one source in the *New York News*.

The struggle to gain access to gun license records went through the courts for years.

The *Wall Street Journal* decided enough was enough and took the case to the Court of Appeals, which delivered a 4-to-3 decision that previously classified pistol permits are public documents.

When the story broke in 1981, the public discovered that 29,000 elite New Yorkers were allowed to carry guns. Among them were the ultra-wealthy Laurance Rockefeller, the celebrity William Buckley, paranormal spoon-bender Uri Geller and entertainer Arthur Godfrey.

Among the many denied a permit were singer Frank Sinatra,

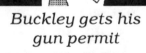

Buckley gets his gun permit

Mets sports figure Rusty Staub, and writer Pete Hamill, who told other media people that he was doing it just to see how hard it was to get one, and there might be a column in it. We're sure he'd never actually carry a gun if he had gotten the permit. You believe that, don't you? Anyway, the breakdown of gun license holders did not look much like a cross-section of average America.

No permit for Ol' Blue Eyes

Here's how it looked on a *New York News* chart.

New York City Gun Permit Holders in 1981 by Profession

Entertainers	5
Doctors	679
Lawyers	349
Newsmen and Editors	9
Executives	276
Brokers	178
Pharmacists	177
Drug Store Operators	18
Gun Custodians	353
Receptionists	124
Corporate Officers	2,078
Other Store Owners	2,878
Dentists	245
Plumbers	44
Miscellaneous	1,104

Well, maybe the Federation had been right about the elitism among New York City pistol permit holders. Yes, there are 44 plumbers and 124 receptions. Yes, there are only 9 newsmen and editors and only 5 entertainers. But 2,078 corporate officers? And 276 executives? And there's not even a listing of politicians, who are presumably lumped into "Miscellaneous."

Have things gotten any more democratic? Not as of 1993, according to the *Boston Globe*. In a story headlined, "Elite in NYC are packing heat."

It appears the list has grown a little longer and a lot more elite. Our old standbys are still there: Laurance Rockefeller and William F. Buckley, Jr. But a new face or two have appeared, and very famous faces at that.

Funnyman Bill Cosby has been granted the privilege of firepower. He was issued the permit in 1988 after stating that he and members of his family had received unspecified death threats.

Donald Trump and Howard Stern also cited death threats and the cops said, okay, here's your license.

And then there is another famous face that's carrying a concealed weapon on the streets of New York. Can we talk?

Joan Rivers has a permit. But, really, can you imagine who would want to attack Joan Rivers? Oh, well, celebrity does have its perks, then, doesn't it?

And, of course, there is always the celebrity who doesn't get a permit. In 1981 it was Frank Sinatra. In 1993 it was singer/actor Harry Connick, Jr. Not only didn't he get a permit, he got a night in jail. He got a pistol from his sister for Christmas. He was 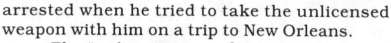 arrested when he tried to take the unlicensed weapon with him on a trip to New Orleans.

The "militarization of the city's cultural elite," as the *Boston Globe* called it, comes at a time when the perception of violence is on the increase in America's cities, said Dr. Gary Kleck, a specialist on American gun culture. Dr. Kleck is the author of the book "Point Blank."

The evidence? Sylvia Heisel, a designer for Barneys New York, created a low-cut, full-length bullet-proof evening gown for the nervous.

Civic leaders, politicians, entertainers, doctors and businessmen pay up to $1,500 a year to target shoot at the exclusive Downtown Rifle and Pistol Club. Director Bill Messick won't say who belongs to his outfit.

One of the more colorful rejects in the gun permit gamble is porn mogul Al Goldstein, the editor and publisher of *Screw* Magazine and producer of the late-night cable show "Midnight Blue." He's been trying to get on the gun carry list since 1978, the year *Hustler* Magazine publisher Larry Flint was crippled by an assailant's bullet. After a string of rejected applications,

Goldstein took his case all the way to the New York State Appeals Court.

He told the *Boston Globe*, "If the crooks and crazies are packing Uzis or MAC-10s, at least let me carry a Beretta." Goldstein is a member of both the American Civil Liberties Union and the National Rifle Association.

Goldstein says he has more reason to need a weapon permit than the others on the list. The 42nd Street massage parlors and downtown sex clubs he frequents to review for his magazine are not only unsavory, he said, they are unsafe. And we innocents thought all those sex shops were supposed to be fun places, Al. Oh, well, it's a dirty job, but I guess somebody has to do it.

Goldstein also said he was pistol whipped by two thugs in his midtown office more than 10 years ago for writing an "unfavorable review" of what he believes is a Mafia-controlled massage parlor. Maybe he needs a permit. The police allow him to keep a licensed .38-caliber revolver in his apartment, but not to carry it.

It's clear that if you're part of the New York City elite, you've got a much better chance of getting a license to carry a gun than the average citizen. Things haven't changed much in the Big Apple for two decades. Tough anti-gun laws. One of the highest crimes rates in the nation. Favoritism to the high and mighty.

> ## With Liberty and Justice for whoever's got the most money and power

How can a city be a hypocrite?
See?

It Ain't the Second Suggestion

A well regulated Militia, being necessary to the security of a free State, the right of the people to keep and bear Arms, shall not be infringed.

Amendment II (1791)
United States Constitution

I'M SURE GLAD HE'S TAKING THE RAP INSTEAD OF US.

D. Raymond Sanford

Outgunned

A humor book on politically correct guns wouldn't be complete without a laugh at ourselves. In this memorable Bill Mauldin cartoon, the media have blasted holes in the National Rifle Association, symbolizing the whole pro-gun movement. Having been on the receiving end of a lot of media mischief myself, I sure know what he means. You just have to grin and bear it. It's the democratic process—messy but best.

Ever wonder what gun owners look like to the media? Me too. I've often thought that the media see even the best, most respectable gun owner as some sort of sweatshirt-and-sneaker-clad barbarian storming the gates of civilization. This Corel cartoon makes the point, although the gun-toter isn't drooling and doesn't have fangs or nine-inch nails.

World Class Hypocrites

Case #5

Anti-gun Columnist
Carl Rowan Pulls a Rambo

June 14, 1988. 2 a.m. In the dark alley-
way, a roving band of youths cruised Northwest
Washington, stealthily seeking an unguarded
swimming pool and maybe even one with a Jacuzzi.

They were "pool hoppers," a shadowy, noto-
rious breed of unruly young people who prowl
wealthy streets in search of a cheap—and unauthorized—dunk.

They came upon the fine home and silently
sneaked around back. Aha! There it was, their
quarry, the Inviting Private Pool—with Jacuzzi.

All the lights in the house were out. The
owner was probably away or sound asleep. This
was their Big Chance.

Over the 8-foot fence and into the Jacuzzi clambered one Benjamin Smith, 18 years old, a resident of Chevy Chase, Maryland, accompanied by his several companions, among them Laura A. Bachman, 19, of Bethesda, Maryland, and maybe a few beers.

Ben, Laura and friends were enjoying themselves in the water when the house lights came on. Then the yard lights. Uh-oh! The pool's owner was coming, and was he miffed!

Ben leaped out of the Jacuzzi in a hurry, dripping wet in his underpants, urging his young companions to do likewise.

The Owner Of The Jacuzzi strode into the night and stood looming before them, silhouetted in the doorway.

You can guess what was probably going through his mind.

Look at those bad kids. They stay up late. They trash my water. They act like they didn't do anything wrong.

One of the kids yelled, "Jeez, he's got a gun."

The Owner Of The Jacuzzi shot Ben Smith, then scurried back into the house to hide. At least that's the way Ben tells it.

The D.C. Pool Shooter, The Jacuzzi Vigilante, The Guardian of the Spurting Waters, was none other than *Washington Post* columnist Carl T. Rowan, a ferociously outspoken advocate of gun control.

This Clint Clone, this shoot-first-and-ask-questions-later Cowboy of the Columns had not long before written these scathing words against Bernhard Goetz, who wounded four teenage thugs on a New York subway:

"The crazy passions of vigilantism are as alive in America today as the AIDS virus...New York's 'subway vigilante' is getting away with a vicious shooting spree because those he shot could be characterized by his defense attorney as 'a wolfpack' and 'savages.' God spare us all a widening spell of lawlessness in which self-styled vigilantes may decide what you and I deserve."

On the other hand, self-styled vigilante Carl Rowan tried to vindicate his actions in a subsequent column titled "At Least They're Not Writing My Obituary" with these words:

"When he kept coming I figured that he must be stoned on marijuana—which police reportedly found around the Jacuzzi—and that he was a threat to my life. After a third warning, with this man perhaps 6 feet from me and the door, he lunged toward me. I fired a shot at his feet ... Let my political enemies ... know that as long as authorities leave this society awash in drugs and guns, I will protect my family."

What a great defense! Charles Bronson would be proud.

Hmm.... Let's see if we've got this straight.

It's okay for Carl Rowan to shoot a guy he thinks poses a threat to his life. But it's not okay for Bernhard Goetz to shoot a guy he thinks poses a threat to his life.

What the heck, that's fair, isn't it? Carl Rowan is a famous and important man, has a big house and a nice pool. He has to protect his family. Nobody ever heard of Bernhard Goetz, who had a little apartment and worked in obscurity. So what if he gets killed or maimed in the subway? That's Rowan Logic. Two plus two equals whatever suits me.

Anyway, Rowan's bullet hit Smith in the wrist. The police took a dim view of Mr. Rowan's actions, and thought a while about charging him with assault, but decided the poor celebrity needed a break, and only charged him with the lesser misdemeanor offenses of possessing an unregistered pistol and ammunition. Conviction could have resulted in a jail term of up to two years and a fine of up to $2,000.

Now, the fact that Rowan had a handgun in a city with the strictest handgun control laws on the books is interesting in itself.

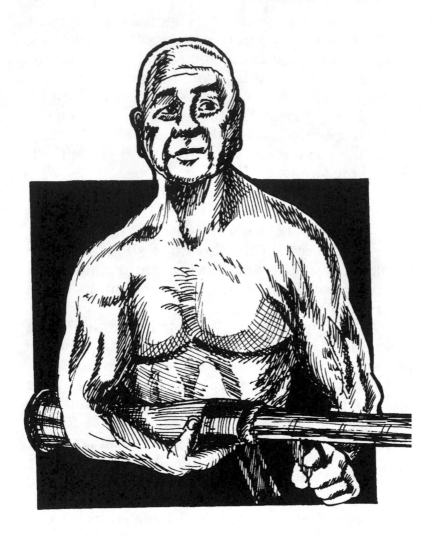

THIS PROPERTY PROTECTED
BY
CARL ROWAN!

Back in 1981, when Nancy Reagan admitted she sometimes slept with a .25-caliber automatic on her bed table, Rowan wrote, "We must reverse this psychology. We can do it by passing a law that says anyone found in possession of a handgun except a legitimate officer of the law goes to jail—period!"

Lofty sentiment, no doubt. But when Carl's psychology matched Nancy's, the Faster Blaster didn't volunteer to do the jail thing for us. Period!

Rambo Rowan's case went to trial September 26, 1988. His defense attorney, Raoul L. Carroll, characterized the pool hopping youths in Carl's back yard as drug-crazed threats to life and property.

A court had earlier dropped illegal entry charges against Ben Smith and Laura Bachman after the two agreed to perform 40 hours of community service, so Rowan's defense attorney didn't make too much of their drug-crazed danger.

Rowan, who was 63 at the time, said that his life had been threatened in the past, and also said that he was confronted by Ben Smith. He said that he warned the youth that he had a gun, but that the youth lunged at him. He fired what he said was a warning shot.

Sounds reasonable.

Clint Eastwood fires warning shots into people's wrists all the time in the Dirty Harry movies. It's a Lone Ranger sort of thing. Just disable your opponent, don't kill him. Very humane.

Then the Rev. Jesse Jackson brought race into the incident—Rowan is an African-American. Some black leaders said they saw racial implications in public reaction to the episode, which ranged from sympathetic support for Rowan to gleeful charges of hypocrisy from pro-gun supporters to angry calls for stricter laws just like Rowan had earlier demanded. I recall supporting Rowan's right to defend himself with a gun at the time, and there was nothing racial about it—I also got a chuckle out of Carl's hypocrisy.

However, Rev. Jackson said that he thought that "a man defending the privacy of his backyard at 2 a.m. is perfectly acceptable behavior," and "that anyone who crawls over an eight-foot fence a 2 a.m. and then does not harken to an appeal to leave is a threat." Who can fault that thinking? I agree with it.

However, Judge Arthur L. Burnett Sr. of the District of Columbia Superior Court allowed evidence of the June 14 events to be admitted, even though the charges against Rowan were only possession of an unregistered pistol and ammunition, which had nothing to do with the shooting itself.

The defense was interesting. Rowan said that the .22-caliber pistol was given to him by his son, Carl T. Rowan Jr., a former agent of the Federal Bureau of Investigation. Rowan and his attorney said that federal agents are not required to register handguns. So Rowan pleaded not guilty.

In the end, the jury was hung by 9 to 3 in Rowan's favor, but could not reach a decision. Judge Burnett ruled a mistrial. Officials decided not to ask for a retrial. So Rambo Rowan walked out a free man, an anti-gun nut with a notch on his own gun.

Conservative Patrick Buchanan, in his role as columnist with Tribune Media Services, enjoyed feeding a serving of crow to Mr. Rowan while wondering if Militia Carl had learned anything from his venture into armed vigilante country.

Buchanan wrote: "The 'society' Carl Rowan describes as failed is a society Carl Rowan helped to create. The 'authorities' who run Washington are, after all, Marion Barry & Co., Rowan's candidates and Rowan's friends. The city's political tone and style are set by *The Washington Post*, where Rowan works; and the capital remains proudly the one political precinct in America to have voted liberal demo-

cratic in the conservative landslides of '72 and '84. Washington is truly the House That Carl Built, along with his liberal friends; and if that city is 'awash in drugs and guns,' whose fault is that? "

Rowan remains unreconstructed and unrepentant. He still spouts anti-gun rhetoric from his newspaper pulpit, blasting the National Rifle Association and other pro-gun groups.

Maybe fate has a sense of humor, though: His son Carl Jr. now works for the NRA's lobbying arm, the Institute for Legislative Action.

World Class Hypocrites

Case #6

Diane Feinstein:
My Gun Permit's OK
Your Gun Permit's Not OK

She was a Pistol Packin' Mama, but she didn't want you to own a handgun. Diane Feinstein is her name, and Senator from California is her game. But back in 1982 she was Mayor of San Francisco. And she decided to stop everyone in her city from owning a handgun like she had owned for many years. So she sponsored a handgun ban similar to one passed earlier by the Illinois village of Morton Grove. And she didn't bat an eyelash about the inconsistency of her position. A typical Gun Grabber.

Two years before Dianne Feinstein took over as mayor of San Francisco—after the murder of Mayor George Moscone by County Supervisor Harvey Milk with a .38-caliber revolver—she got a permit to carry a .38-caliber revolver of her own. It was the only handgun permit issued in San Francisco that year.

In those days Feinstein was a city supervisor. She was the person who found the assassinated Moscone and put a finger through a bullet hole trying to get a pulse. She claimed that the experience prompted her to ban handguns in San Francisco.

Feinstein got her handgun permit and was trained in its use "when I had terrorist attacks by the New World Liberation Front, with a bomb at my house, when my husband was dying, when I had windows shot out."

All very good reasons to own a handgun. All very good reasons for Dianne Feinstein to own a handgun. But if you ever have any troubles in San Francisco, you'll never have a good enough reason to defend yourself from deadly force, thanks to Good Ol' Don't-Do-As-I-Do, Do-As-I-Say Dianne.

In her early arguments for the gun ban, Mayor Feinstein said, "San Francisco now has the highest *per capita* homicide rate of any city in California. Clearly, we must stop this carnage."

Who could disagree? Stopping crime is good for everyone. But does Do-Gooder Dianne want to stop criminals by more severe sentences for actual criminals? No! She wants to prevent law abiding citizens from having the means to defend themselves from those criminals.

Her proposed law would make possession of handguns a misdemeanor punishable by 30 days in jail. Citizens would have 90 days to sell the weapons or surrender them to police with no questions asked. Police and military personnel were exempt.

'Let's Cool it until the Police strikes end'

Famous 1979 Bill Mauldin political cartoon on the hypocrisies of gun control nuts.

The ban in the city and county—they have the same boundaries—of 750,000 people (at that time) would not extend to rifles or shotguns.

Feinstein's proposal set off a firestorm of protest. Her hypocrisy was deemed "revolting" by State Senator H.L. Richardson. "Mayor Feinstein once admittedly carried a gun for protection. Today for her protection she has security guards paid for by the taxpayers of San Francisco."

Pro-gun forces asserted that the ban was illegal. However, the Morton Grove ban, upon which Feinstein's measure was modeled, had been challenged in U.S. District Court but was upheld. An appeal also failed, and the U.S. Supreme Court refused to hear the case.

The San Francisco Board of Supervisors had passed a tough gun registration law in 1968, but it was immediately blocked by the courts. The State Legislature later passed a law that preempted local gun laws in San Francisco and Beverly Hills. Things didn't look good for gun owners.

Chief attorney Peter Keane of the city's public defender's office advised Feinstein that while the codes forbid local governments in California from requiring the licensing or registration of pistols, they do not apply to an outright weapons ban.

Feinstein as much as admitted that gun control laws do not work—"I don't anticipate this will stop the problem. But what we aim to do is stop the access to the problem."

Morton Grove had the embarrassing experience of having only 12 of an estimated 3,100 handguns in the town turned in to the police after its ban went into effect.

Feinstein's gun ban passed the sharply divided city Board of Supervisors on a 6-4 vote and she signed it into law June 28, 1982. The Second Amendment Foundation immediately filed suit questioning Keane's opinion about preemption.

District Attorney Arlo Smith made it clear that he would not even charge anyone with violating the new ban until its validity had been determined by the courts.

Police officials also made clear that they would enforce the law only in the course of their normal work; there would be no house-to-house searches for illicit handguns.

Despite the furor, the gun ban stuck.

The bottom line was, after all the legal dust settled, the people of San Francisco kept their right to own a handgun and Diane Feinstein lost her court battle.

Aide to Senator Boxer Arrested for Gun
—Just after the lawmaker had introduced a bill to ban assault weapons

In July 1993, a receptionist at Senator Barbara Boxer's San Francisco office was arrested for carrying a 9mm semiautomatic and 15 rounds of ammunition. The arrest of Roger Calderon was announced just hours after Boxer had made an impassioned plea on the floor of the Senate for a ban on assault weapons like the ones Gian Luigi Ferri used to kill eight people and injure six others only two weeks earlier at the posh office building known as 101 California Street.

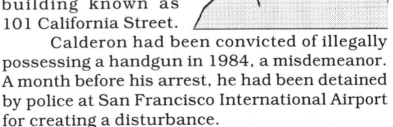

Calderon had been convicted of illegally possessing a handgun in 1984, a misdemeanor. A month before his arrest, he had been detained by police at San Francisco International Airport for creating a disturbance.

When arrested after Boxer's speech for gun bans, Calderon told officers he was connected with the CIA, had been conducting research on UFOs and needed the gun for protection. Wow! That blasts us out of the Hypocrisy Zone and back into the familiar, ordinary world of the Twilight Zone.

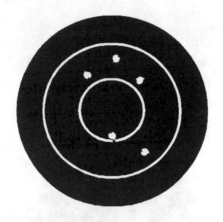

Part Two

It's the Stupidity, Stupid

Alan's Dictionary: **stu•pid** *adj* : slow of mind; given to unintelligent decisions or acts : UN-IMAGINATIVE, OBTUSE, UNFEELING, like the gun control crowd that can't see the results of disarming law-abiding citizens in a world that always produces a few bad apples who use guns to commit crimes.

There's nothing sillier than disarming our society with anti-gun laws which crooks never obey. Waiting periods give criminals a grace period for murder, gun turn-ins merely help gun manufacturers sell new guns, gun bans prompt gun-buying rushes— stupid, stupid, stupid.

Gun control instead of criminal control has to be the Mother of All Stupidity.

World Class Dumb-downs

Case #1

It's Gun Control, Bill

Bill Clinton campaigned against stupidity while running for President ("It's the Economy, Stupid!"), but once he got in office, he himself dumbed down the debate over guns.

He tried to look like a pro-gun guy when he went on that famous duck hunting trip to Maryland's Eastern Shore with eight notables, including two pro-gun congressmen, Representatives Bill Brewster (D-OK) and John Dingell (D-MI).

Clinton told United Press International reporters that he had hunted and shot guns since he was a little boy. He noted that hunting is a part of the national culture and "an important part of the life of millions." He even got himself picketed by animal rights activists before leaving the White House on the hunting trip.

The Prez insisted he was not against the possession of hunting rifles and shotguns, but called for a ban on semi-automatic firearms and all private handgun ownership.

What's wrong with this picture?

Simple: While he accepts the "sporting use" criterion for firearms ownership, he rejects the "self-defense" reason. As the bumper sticker reminds us, the Second Amendment ain't about duck hunting.

Now, it could be that, with more Secret Service agents than hunting companions in that cozy private lodge in Maryland, Bill Clinton didn't feel particularly in danger. But it's more likely that his brain cells go south anytime somebody suggests that the government can't do it all—no matter what "all" might be.

Well, Bill, the real world doesn't provide us all with bodyguards who have been trained to take the bullet for us.

And the real world also doesn't come with criminals who obey anti-gun laws.

That's a sore point with most of us gun owners. We simply can't grasp how anyone in their right mind could for a single minute believe that criminals are going to obey gun laws.

Yo, Bill! Criminals are people who break the law! Remember from law school? Criminals? They break the law. That's why they're criminals.

Earth to Planet Clinton....

Do you read me, Bill?

Crooks aren't going to obey anti-gun laws!

Only law-abiding citizens will obey, and your anti-gun laws will disarm them, Bill.

Bill?

" WE'LL HIT THE LIQUOR STORE ON 48TH...THEN SHOOT UP THE QUIK MART
BY THE INTERSTATE... THEN MAYBE LOOK FOR A FEW HOSTAGES...
FIRST, THOUGH, WE'LL HAVE TO STOP BY A LICENSED GUN DEALER AND
REGISTER OUR FIREARMS.

The cartoonist gets it.
Why doesn't the President?

I'm sorry, but it can get dangerous out here.
And we each have a fundamental right to self-de-
fense, both morally and legally. You're a lawyer,
Bill—think about the self-defense argument.
Or are you going to ban that too?
Are we entitled to speculate on why the Chief
Executive feels so anti-gun?
No?
Well, let's do it anyway.
President Clinton's anti-gun feelings may
stem from a traumatic childhood event, according
to a book and a magazine interview.
The scene haunts him still. He was barely
five years old when his stepfather, Roger Clinton,
fired a gun at his mother, Virginia Kelley. The

bullet smashed into a wall next to where Kelley was seated.

"I remember that incident vividly, like it was yesterday," Clinton said in a personal, frank interview in *Good Housekeeping* magazine.

"That bullet could have ricocheted and done anything," Clinton recalled. "It could have killed me. If anything had happened, Roger would never have gotten over it."

Roger was Virginia's second husband. Her first, William Blythe, was killed in a car accident before Bill Clinton was born.

An unauthorized biography, *Clinton Confidential*, by George Carpozi, Jr., told the same story, and described how the incident first came to light. Clinton, during his presidential campaign, was very cagey about hiding his past, annoying reporters. Several instead interviewed his mother.

At times, Mrs. Kelley told them, her second husband was a violent drunk.

New York magazine's Joe Klein picked up on that in his interview with Clinton, who finally relented to talk about the early years—and to recognize the bullet hole incident.

"I remember once when I was four or five and he was screaming at my mother, and he actually fired a gun in the house. There was a bullet hole in the wall. It could have ricocheted, hit my mother, hit me. I ran out of the room. I had to live with that bullet hole, look at it every day."

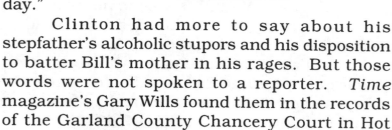

Clinton had more to say about his stepfather's alcoholic stupors and his disposition to batter Bill's mother in his rages. But those words were not spoken to a reporter. *Time* magazine's Gary Wills found them in the records of the Garland County Chancery Court in Hot Springs, Arkansas.

"I was present on March 27, 1959, and it was I who called my mother's attorney, who in turn had to get the police to come to the house to arrest the defendant."

Bill made that statement to his stepfather's attorney at a deposition hearing held sometime in 1961. He was 15 at the time. The proceeding was precipitated by Mrs. Clinton's decision to take no more abuse from her husband and to divorce him.

With this story circulating widely now, imagine all the psycho-babble we're going to hear about guns in the home.

But think too how this incident might have influenced the judgment of the man once he got to the White House. Is an early childhood trauma blotting out your gun rights?

Senator Gets Mugged

Anti-gun U.S. Senator Barbara Mikulski (D-MD) was mugged outside her Baltimore home and dislocated her hand while defending herself, her office reported in 1995.

The Maryland Democrat had parked her car at about 11:45 p.m. on a Sunday in mid-October and was heading to her house when she was approached by a man in a blue sweatsuit. He knocked her down, stole her purse and fled, police officer Robert Weinhold said.

"He pushed her to take the purse. She pushed him back" and fell to the ground, said Rachel Kunzler, a spokeswoman for the senator.

Mikulski, 59, was treated for a dislocated hand at Mercy Medical Center and released. Mikulski canceled one of her three appointments the next day to get follow-up treatment at Union Memorial Hand Clinic.

"She's feeling much better," Kunzler said.

The Senator has lived all her life in the Fells Point area, a well-known tourist destination along Baltimore's waterfront.

Police said the purse was recovered a block away. About $40 in cash and an undetermined amount in Traveler's Checks were missing.

Well, Senator, this is another case where a good common-sense self-defense like a handgun would have come in handy.

Things That Don't Bear
Too Close Examination

Sigmund Freud wrote in his *Introductory Lectures on Psychoanalysis* that "A fear of weapons is a sign of retarded sexual and emotional maturity."

Then consider what the shrink would do in the 1994 case of the man from El Cerrito, California, who turned in a shotgun to police as part of a novel two-month-long program of "Therapy-for-Guns."

The 110-member Contra Costa Psychological Association offered therapy vouchers to people who brought unloaded guns in to local law enforcement agencies. At the going rate, the single taker got a voucher worth $300. That's three hours at a hundred bucks an hour.

Do you think these shrinks tried to get their patient to grow up sexually and emotionally? Think the psychologists tried to cure his "fear of weapons?" Or their own?

Of course not. They're part of the mental health industry that *creates* fear of weapons, not cures it. Fear is good business.

Freud was known for his blunt honesty. Modern psychologists seem to have acquired a different reputation.

The Born Loser, a popular cartoon strip, perfectly catches the stupidity of many gun control measures.

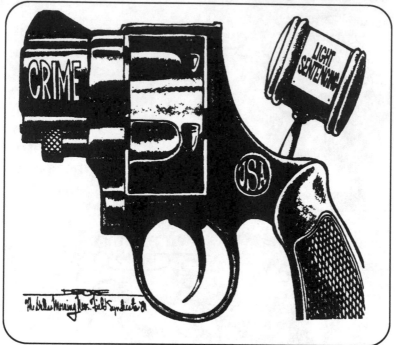

Criminal Control Anyone?

The *Dallas Morning News* is not usually pro-gun, but this political cartoon from its pages comes close. Even though the snub-nosed revolver is labelled "Crime," the hammer that falls to send the bullet flying is "Light Sentencing."

Not so stupid after all.

You can still see an anti-gun bias lurking in the choice of a handgun to represent crime. The self-defense part of gun ownership remains out of sight. This big and important Texas newspaper hasn't quite made the intuitive leap to common sense self-defense.

Well, even if it's not exactly pro-gun, at least it's anti-criminal.

Serious Stupidity Award

Gun Bans

The whole idea of banning guns instead of dealing with people who misuse them is so stupid I'm making a single blanket award for Serious Stupidity to all governments that have banned guns.

But I won't copout, so I'll give a specific Dumb-Dumb Award to the District of Columbia.

In 1977, Washington, D.C. enacted the nation's toughest gun law, which virtually prohibits the private possession of handguns.

By 1984, D.C.'s homicide rate had increased 30 percent. Its robbery rate by then was up 62 %. Even the District's Assistant Chief of Police said, "I personally don't think gun control laws work." No kidding.

Things haven't improved yet.

Then why do governments keep writing laws that don't work? There are over 22,000 gun laws in this country, and there is no evidence that any of them has succeeded.

A comparison of state firearm laws to their crime rates shows no lower rates in strict gun control states.

Which leads a rational person to a rather simple conclusion: Criminals and psychopaths will always find a way to get guns, regardless of controls.

Is that too hard to figure out?

What's the lesson of New York City? Despite one of the toughest gun laws— in effect for over 75 years—there are an estimated 1 to 2 million illegal handguns in the Big Apple.

In the District of Columbia, less than 1% of the firearms confiscated from criminals by the police are legally registered.

There's better evidence that indicates strict sentencing is a more effective crime control step. Use a gun, go to jail. If you're in jail, you can't victimize the citizenry.

The cartoon below figured it out.

Then why do the press and politicians tell

....THAT'S
WHY I STARTED
WORKING
DAYS

you it's dangerous to keep a handgun for protection?

Yet handguns are used by tens of thousands of honest, decent people who use them to defend life and property.

Consider these vignettes from real life:

The New York cabbie who killed a robber with his handgun—

The lady lawyer in Baltimore who drew a pistol from her purse to thwart a holdup—

The retired electrician who shot two vandals after they'd stabbed him 25 times—

And the Chicago woman who stopped a knife-wielding rapist with her gun.

Do these stories make headlines?

Not often.

So you see, when I talk about Gun Rights, I'm talking about Civil Rights. Guns don't have rights. People have rights. The right to defend your life and property is pretty basic. The right to keep and bear arms is about as rock-bottom as it gets for self-protection.

Maybe that's too simple.

Maybe that's why politicians keep passing gun control laws instead of criminal control laws.

Whatever the reason, here's my Serious Stupidity Award to all the governments that have passed gun bans.

Dumb.

Really Dumb.

The Police Can't Be Everywhere

Most police departments are truly public defenders and do their best to protect the citizens. The fact that they can't be everywhere to protect everyone seems to escape gun control advocates. As this political cartoon shows, however, some police departments have stained their reputations by incidents such as the L.A.P.D. Rodney King beating captured on videotape by a passerby.

Sometimes It's Just As Well

The point actually made by the Los Angeles Police Department in the Rodney King case might not be the one the police had in mind, but it did convince a newspaper cartoonist that self-defense with a gun might not be a bad idea.

Anti-gun nuts *can* come to their senses. All it takes is getting mugged or watching the L.A.P.D. on videotape out there protecting the public.

What Really Happens
With A Gun Ban?

The rocket scientists in our government haven't figured out a lot of things, but they should have noticed by now that the first thing people do when a new gun ban is announced is to run out and buy a lot of guns before it goes into effect.

Bill Clinton's 1993 "Crime Bill" (and it *was* a crime) banned a lot of sporting guns that somehow got classified as "assault weapons."

Before they could even vote on this anti-gun bill, the mere threat of it sent thousands of people scurrying to buy guns. The rush was so huge even the rabidly anti-gun *New York Times* ran a story on it.

In late December of 1993, *Times* reporter Drummond B. Ayres, Jr. filed a story with an interesting premise:

"Frightened by a spate of mass shootings and other seemingly random crimes, and worried that new gun-control laws may make it all but impossible to obtain a firearm for self-defense or recreational use, many Americans are rushing to buy pistols, rifles and shotguns."

What a surprise! Gee, this never happened before, did it?

The only people surprised were those who had been living in a cave on Mars for the past twenty years!

Firearms dealers spoke in informal interviews from coast to coast, all reporting a surge in sales, often to record levels.

Manufacturers said they were having trouble keeping up with demand from retailers, and, as a result, prices for some guns soared.

Many purchasers said they had never considered owning a gun until the carnage left by recent mass shootings in places like New York, California and Colorado starkly focused their attention on the nation's crime problem.

They were finally moved to make a purchase, they said, upon learning that Congress had passed one gun control law, the Brady Bill, and that President Clinton was pushing for other laws.

"I wanted to be able to come and get it when I wanted to get it," said Diana Skaggs, a secretary shopping at Greer Gun and Pawn in Greer, South Carolina. She paid $401 for two boxes of bullets and a 9mm pistol, the first firearm she has ever owned.

" A THREE-DAY COOLING OFF PERIOD!? DOES THE TWO DAYS I'VE BEEN IN LINE COUNT ? "

Personal safety had become a personal issue with Skaggs, and not just because of recent mass slayings and other criminal violence around the country.

A few nights previous, in her own neighborhood, she heard a man screaming out in the darkness for help.

Other gun buyers, mainly collectors and recreational shooters, said they were rushing to make a purchase because they feared new regulations being proposed might outlaw or sharply curtail sales of the particular kinds of firearms they wanted or because they anticipated such firearms would become a good investment.

"I collect guns and I'm trying to beat out the President before he makes it so I can't get one," said Nathan Ellis, a heating and air-conditioning installer from Jacksonville, Arkansas, while cradling a newly purchased assault rifle at Don's Weaponry in North Little Rock.

He described the purchase as "an investment," noting that the gun he had just bought for $269 had been selling for $179 several weeks earlier.

The *Times* noted there are no comprehensive national figures on just how much gun sales have surged over the past few months. But a random sampling of gun dealers across the country produced numerous reports of month-to-month increases of 50, 60 and even 100%.

"Sales have skyrocketed," said John Kayson, manager of Rick's Gun & Sport in Lockport, Illinois, a town 35 miles southwest of Chicago. "We're having trouble getting guns from distributors."

"Crime is obviously a factor," he said, "But people also are afraid of all this talk of regulation."

At the Alamo Gun Shop in Houston, sales were running about 50% ahead of the level recorded a year earlier.

"We have a lot of first-time victims who were anti-gun, or not really pro-gun, who come in for protection, said Judy Chmiel, the owner. She added that many purchasers tell her, "I'm going to buy it before they tell me I can't buy it."

At Don's Weaponry in North Little Rock, Don Hill, the owner, reported that he had sold 75 guns the past week compared with about 25 guns during the same week a year earlier.

"Honest citizens are buying my guns. Criminals are getting them off the streets. The Brady Bill doesn't affect them at all. It only hurts the good guys."

"Last month was the best for sales that I have experienced in the eight years I've been in business," Hill said. "Overall, business this year has been twice as good as last year."

But whatever the true crime rate in the nation and however mild the new gun laws may be, many Americans said their fear about crime is increasing, as is their worry about gun control, particularly since Clinton followed up passage of the Brady Bill with a proposal to license gun owners next.

"I hate to sound like a cliché, but if you outlaw guns, only outlaws will have them," said Pete Ramirez as he and his wife shopped for a pistol at B&B Sales in North Hollywood, California. "But I can tell you one thing: If they break into my house and I shoot them, they won't be coming back."

"I WISH THEY'D PASS GUN CONTROL. IT'S GETTING SO YOU DON'T FEEL SAFE BREAKING INTO A HOUSE ANYMORE!"

Special Dummy Award

The Gun Buyback Program

No one seems to know exactly what genius invented the "gun buyback" program that popped up across the country a few years ago, but it has to be the dumbest thing since gun bans.

The general idea is this: A law enforcement agency puts out a public notice that it will accept guns turned in by any citizen, no questions asked.

There are several variations. In the cheapest case, the police don't buy, they simply offer an amnesty to the person turning in the weapon.

In most cases, there is an actual buy-back, a money reward, usually donated by a private company. Turn in your old gun, get money. It sounds like a great way to get some chump to pay for that rusty old inoperable and worthless shotgun that grandpa left in the attic after his grandfather left it to him as a "priceless heirloom."

Only the chump in the gun buyback program is usually the taxpayer, who gets stuck with the fallout.

Sometimes the cost is beyond calculation. Like the New Jersey murder using a gun purchased with $50 received in a Camden County gun buyback two days earlier.

Camden County was the first in New Jersey to initiate a guns-for-cash program. It doesn't always pay to be first in line.

One of the three teenagers charged in the killing of a 31-year-old man told police that the $50 used to buy a .25-caliber pistol from a stranger on the street was money from the police. The youth got the money from authorities when a "possibly inoperable" old shotgun was turned in during Camden's January, 1994 10-day amnesty gun buyback program.

David Perry, Jr., was shot to death with a gun bought in front of the police mini-station at 27th and Federal Streets in Camden—bought presumably from a man who was just about to turn it in. Is that ironic, or what?

One or more of the three teenagers involved bought the semiautomatic handgun on the last day of the gun turn-in program. Perry was killed two days later as he walked to catch a bus to his job as a nursing assistant in a Woodbury, New Jersey, nursing home.

Charged in the killing were Sean Barge, 18, and two 15-year-old boys, one from Camden, the other from Salem.

The three teenagers were standing on the corner of South 36th and Freemont Streets in Camden at 4 a.m. on January 28, 1994, when they decided to rob the next person to walk by, police detectives said.

Perry happened to be that person. The teenagers fled empty handed to a nearby house, but police followed their footprints in the snow and arrested the three. The handgun was found at the house, police said.

Camden County Prosecutor Edward F. Borden Jr. said, "We have checked out the information and there were two sawed-off shotguns turned in that day. One was brought in by a woman and the other was given to authorities by a man. The names of the donors don't match those of the people charged in the murder."

The prosecutor admitted, however, that it was entirely possible that the youth charged had turned in one of the shotguns—people who turned in guns for $50 were not required to present identification (it's an amnesty, you know), or to write down their names. Some even gave the name of George D. Pugh, Camden's chief of police. Now that's gallows humor.

The prosecutor defended the buy back program, even though it had killed a man. "There are 35,000 guns manufactured in the United States every day," Borden said. The 10-day program had helped cut the number of guns on the streets.

It cut the number of people, too.

But there's another part of the buyback program that's so crazy it's hard to believe.

I didn't make this up. Honest.

In Contra Costa County, California, several police agencies spent $20,000 to buy and destroy guns. But Contra Costa County Sheriff Richard Rainey refused to participate in a five city gun buyback program and instead sold off seized guns to raise twice that much.

Rainey signed a contract with the Modesto auctioneer firm of Ernst & Associates, who bought them for resale to the public. The money received was added to the department's $64 million budget.

Rainey argued that gun buybacks do little to reduce crime.

"I don't think the gun amnesty programs really get guns off the street, not guns that are being used by criminals." Sheriff Rainey said. "Generally, they are guns in someone's closet, just guns that they want to get rid of."

Rainey said Contra Costa County used to dump its confiscated firearms at sea or send them to be crushed.

Rainey noted that selling confiscated firearms to honest citizens could help ease the impact of a $2.5 million budget cut in his department.

Local anti-gun politicians were not happy.

In some states, such as Washington, the law requires that seized guns be auctioned off to help the state budget. As the cartoon on the next page shows, a Seattle Post Intelligencer newspaper cartoonist had a low opinion of the situation.

To get a flavor of the quality of the debate over gun turn-ins and gun buy backs, let's go to Maryland in June of 1995.

Here we'll meet the person credited (wrongly) with starting the gun turn-in idea.

A gun control crusader named Julie Elseroad founded a group called Enough Is Enough Inc. in 1991 after a student brought a .357-caliber Magnum gun to her son's middle school.

"October 23, 1991—that day changed my life," she said.

Because of her appearances on national television, Elseroad's idea of turning in guns caught on throughout the country, she says.

Thousands of weapons have been turned in as a result, she says.

Elseroad's Enough Is Enough is a Silver Spring-based non-profit gun control organization that states its purpose as "violence prevention and education." Elseroad, however, doesn't push switchblade turn-ins, incendiary device turn-ins, bomb turn-ins, baseball bat turn-ins— or turn-ins of any other object commonly used in violent acts. She's strictly gun control, but puts a nice spin on what she calls it.

Elseroad also knows how to play the human interest card to the hilt. She frequently tells the media the story of how a woman came to one of her gun turn-ins and handed over a gun, then collapsed in Elseroad's arms sobbing.

"At first I thought it was hard for her to get rid of it," said Elseroad.

"No, you don't understand," the woman said.

"I told her I was sorry and asked her what it was that she had to tell me. Then she told me that her husband had committed suicide with that gun."

That's a gut punch.

Who could fail to feel the grief and agony of the woman in this story? We all feel the pain.

But what's that got to do with the purpose of Elseroad's gun turn-ins?

Nothing!

How likely is it that this poor woman's husband would be alive today if she had only turned in the gun before the man killed himself with it?

Not likely at all. Suicide is not exactly your spur-of-the-moment impulse. The lack of a gun hasn't stopped suicides from using knives, razor blades, poison, jumping off cliffs, driving into bridge embankments—and on and on and on.

It's sad that a gun that got turned in had been used in a suicide, but making that fact a part of the debate is to use a classic fallacy.

In rhetoric, the trick even has a fancy name: *synecdoche* (it's pronounced sin-EK-dough-kee). It means to hold out a part as if it were the whole.

Elseroad holds out one gun with terrible association to give all guns terrible associations. Melodramatic, but phony.

I call it the Bloody Shirt Syndrome. Blame the gun.

And it's so crass, using a fallacy to play on the sympathies of the audience to further her cause while exploiting the grief of a distraught widow.

These gun grabbers.... Whew!

Well, Elseroad's group sponsored a one-day gun turn-in program at 16 sites in the Maryland suburbs of Washington, D.C. in mid-1995. Local law enforcement agencies and the Have a Heart Business Alliance cosponsored the event.

It was one of those no-pay, just-turn-your-gun-in deals. An amnesty. Turn your gun in anonymously and voluntarily. Founder Elseroad said "This is a no-questions asked program," she said. No questions and no cash.

For each gun turned in, the Have a Heart Business Alliance donated $25 to the Division of Child Protection at Children's Hospital.

The group had run similar turn-ins during the previous two years, netting 600 guns and hundreds of pounds of ammunition.

Police asked that weapons be placed in a container or clear plastic bag and be transported in the trunk of a vehicle. The ammunition should be kept in a separate part of the vehicle, police asked.

All of the guns in this program were destroyed. In years past, police had taken the guns to the Bethlehem Steel plant in Baltimore for meltdown.

In 1995, the barrels of the guns were sealed with a blow torch and used to help make a 16-foot statue of a plowshare, to be erected at the John Marshall Plaza in Washington.

Critics of the program pointed out that

people who turn in gun are law abiding citizens, like the poor widowed lady, not criminals.

Police and Elseroad defended the program. One cop, Montgomery County police Sgt. Kathleen Brown, a 15-year veteran, said she has responded to many domestic calls where guns have been used during crimes of passion.

"To me, anything we get off the street is significant," Brown told reporters. "We are preventing somebody from stealing a gun out of a home during a burglary and using it on the street."

Wait a minute.

I think I missed something there.

Yes, if you turn in a gun, a burglar can't steal it from you.

But how does that translate into *preventing* crime on the street?

The criminal who intends to use a gun on the street will be *prevented* from getting a gun by the turn-in program?

No, of course not. But such a pubic relations argument is an old trick in debate, another fallacy in rhetoric, called the "missing middle term."

Here's how it works: First, you state something that's clearly true. Everybody agrees with you.

"If you turn in your gun, nobody can steal it from you." Obvious. True. I agree.

Then you leap over an important fact that isn't there, and claim you have proven some marvellous phony conclusion.

You conclude that the burglar who can't steal your gun will be prevented from using a gun on the street. What's wrong with this picture?

My youngest child could tell you: The burglar can go into the next house and steal a gun there. Or buy one on the street. Or get one from a friend. Or.... The list goes on.

The gun turn-in has nothing whatever to do with criminals getting guns. It may indeed prevent a criminal from getting a *specific* gun, but it has zero effect on a criminal getting a gun.

Zero.

A gun supporter in Maryland, Billie J. Grey, sent a letter to the editor in reply to the newspaper story about Elseroad's 1995 gun turn-in and Sgt. Brown's logical leap.

Billie had this to say: "Gun turn-in programs are not new. What Ms. Elseroad has done that is new is that all firearms turned in to the "Enough Is Enough" program are destroyed. All of them are destroyed.

Is it responsible to destroy firearms without checking to see if they were stolen? Is it responsible to destroy firearms without checking to see if they are crime guns? Is it responsible to destroy firearms without determining if they have historic value?

There are museums and parks which can use some of these firearms for display purposes. These museums would be willing to agree never to sell the firearm if they stopped using it in a display.

Even if only one firearm that could be returned to its rightful owner, was used in an enforcement action, or has historic value, is destroyed, the program is not responsible.

Also, is it responsible to encourage people to rely solely on the police for self-defense? Montgomery County police Sgt. Kathleen Brown has been quoted as having responded to many domestic calls where guns have been used during crimes of passion.

She does not mention whether she has responded to calls where the victim was killed or seriously injured after calling 911 but before the police arrived. She does not mention whether she has responded to calls where the intended victim halted the crime by self-defense with a firearm. Perhaps she would have mentioned it had she been asked.

Sgt. Brown is quoted as saying, "We are preventing somebody from stealing a gun out of a home during a burglary and using it on the street." Surely the penalty for burglary is to be paid by the burglar rather than the potential victim. Sgt. Brown's approach to firearms ownership will leave the intended victim without an effective means for lawful self-defense.

Finally, used firearms have value. There are dealers listed in the yellow pages who can give an estimate of the value. To be certain that the price quoted is fair, the owner may get quotes from different dealers. Surely it is responsible to find out how much a firearm is worth before "turning it in" for destruction.

Billie, gun owners thank you for a dose of common sense about gun turn-ins.

The gun buyback idea spread like a virus. Police departments all over the country tried them. In Alabama, the state Senate's Finance and Taxation Committee on a voice vote approved

an unbalanced education budget that included—
for the first time—$100,000 to buy guns back
from school children.

But trouble showed up quickly in the wake
of the buyback programs. In 1994, the Connecticut state government found that a local gun
buyback program needed a bailout. It faced a
deficit of about $280,000 in taxpayer money to
cover a shortfall in what was supposed to be a
privately funded program.

Oops!

A group of Connecticut retailers had earlier in the year offered to provide gift certificates
to people who turned in their guns. It was a
"goods-for-guns" deal, not a "cash-for-guns"
deal. But because of an unexpectedly high response rate, state officials ran out of donated
certificates after seven days and cancelled the
program.

Because 3,000 people who turned in guns
received nothing in return, several state officials,
including Governor Lowell Weicker Jr., proposed
a bailout.

This move displeased a number of folks,
among them Connecticut state Senator George
Gunther and a housewife named Cynthia
Enama, a working mother with two children. The
two of them filed suit in Milford Superior Court
to block the bailout plan.

Gunther argued that state officials have
no authority to transfer public funds to a private program, at least not without approval of
the legislature. The money was being transferred
from an account that provided property tax re-
lief for veterans.

"That's been my concern from the get-go," said House Minority Leader Edward Krawiecki, a Republican from Bristol. "It's not appropriate to use public money for this."

The suit sought a temporary injunction to prevent state officials from using $281,065 in public funds to reimburse former gunowners until the suit was resolved, and a permanent court order banning the use of taxpayer money.

However, the state government continued purchasing gift certificates and distributing them to residents while awaiting the outcome of the court case.

So much for Connecticut's troubles.

Then the Fort Worth, Texas, Police Department discontinued its gun buyback program because it didn't work—meaning that not many people gave up their guns.

In May of 1994, City Manager Bob Terrell said 115 firearms had been purchased since the program's beginning on April 3, 1993. An additional 25 firearms were donated. That's not much of a haul for a turn-in project.

Compared with similar programs in other states, Fort Worth's "Stop the Violence/Stop the Tears" program was a failure, Terrell said.

He noted that in Buffalo, New York, 1,367 guns were turned in over four days in 1993.

In St. Louis, 7,459 guns were turned in within a month in 1991.

"Different programs work in different ways," Terrell commented. "It has been successful in some cities and hasn't been successful in others."

Fort Worth was the first Texas city to establish the program. General Dynamics, now Lockheed Fort Worth Company, donated $25,000 for the gun purchases. About $2,600 was spent and the remainder was to go toward other police programs, Terrell said.

On the day just before Terrell announced that the Fort Worth buy-back was being discontinued, 46 guns were turned in during a similar program in nearby Dallas.

Pro-gunners are divided on what to say when asked about the gun buybacks. However, one response that's guaranteed to anger the gun control crowd is to praise the turn-ins as an excellent way to help gun manufacturers sell new guns by taking used guns out of circulation.

Smile.

Now, if all of this about gun buybacks doesn't sound dumb enough so far, here's one for the books. For this book, at least.

In early 1993, the sponsors of Omaha, Nebraska's gun amnesty program expanded the buyback option to *toy guns*.

I'm not making this up.

The sponsors were the City of Omaha, the Greater Omaha Chamber of Commerce, the Mad Dads, the Omaha Police and Fire Departments, and the Douglas County Attorney's Office.

Their usual buyback deal was to turn in real guns for a $50 voucher. They had netted 315 firearms with this program a month earlier.

Then Mayor Morgan of Omaha got the brainy idea of offering the public to turn in toy guns for $1.

A buck for your kid's water pistol.

Uh-huh.

The local cartoonist had a field day.

Mayor Morgan was The Grinch who stole little Timmy's water pistol for a lousy buck.

Mayor Morgan explained himself thus: "Gun, real and toy, are a danger to the community when they are used in the wrong way. With the toy gun amnesty, we are trying to instill a knowledge that guns and violence have no place in our community."

Get that?

"Guns and violence have no place in our community.

I can see violence having no place in their community.

But guns?

"Guns have no place in our community."

You were elected Mayor of Omaha, Mr. Morgan, not Dictator.

"Guns have no place in our community."

Even the local newspaper, which is not known for its pro-gun editorials, couldn't swallow that one. The Evening World-Herald featured this commentary in its top spot on the Editorial Page on February 8, 1993:

"Reasonable people can debate whether play with toy guns is better of worse than other childhood activities. The fact remains that millions of children have played games of cowboy, soldier or cops-and-robbers—games that provided adventure, stimulated young imaginations and required running, climbing and other healthy activity. The vast majority of those kids grew up to become responsible adults.

"It won't make street gangs less appealing to wannabes if someone hands out dollar bills for the plastic dueling pistols with which kids

First the toy guns, next, the cowboy movies

play at being pirates. Or for the make-believe blasters popularized in the 'Star Wars' movies. Or for scaled-down toy flintlocks that were stored years ago when the Davy Crockett craze was over.

"It won't reduce the drive-by shootings and armed assaults that occur when drug dealers fight turf wars. Nor will it end the horrible accidents that happen all too often when a child comes upon a loaded gun.

"Violence occurs because people are raised without the values that families, schools and churches once instilled—and because society has done too little to get firearms out of the hands of people who will use them irresponsibly. None of those problems will be solved by paying for unwanted toys."

Speaking of unwanted toys, did you hear about the 1995 case of the 16-year-old Vandalia, Illinois, boy who was sentenced to a year's probation and 80 hours of community service for shooting a water gun at St. Elmo High School teacher Mary Jane Mattix? She sought criminal charges.

The news clipping didn't say if they melted down the water gun.

Family values, Granny-Get-Your-Gun Style

From the Historical Files

Little Gems of Dumb

The year was 1974. Mrs. Angelina Alioto disagreed with her husband on the value of a firearm. Her husband was Joseph Alioto, mayor of San Francisco, who often said that handguns should be available only to the police, but that people who were concerned for their safety "can keep a rifle in the house."

Mrs. Alioto ran away from home for 18 days because of her husband's neglect of her, she said. "From 25 to 27 nights in a month, I'm alone here with just my housekeeper. I'm not even allowed to have a gun."

Is that spouse abuse?

About the same time in 1974, the son of television and movie comedian Dean Martin was arrested by federal agents. It seems that Dean Martin, Jr., known as "Dino," had illegal possession of eight machine guns and an antitank gun, or at least that's what the federal grand jury thought when they indicted him in Los Angeles for unlawful possession of firearms. The 22-year-old arsenal owner was released on $5,000 bond. Those movie people!

And those TV people. In 1974, there was a popular cop series on the little screen called "Hawaii-Five-O." It starred actor Jack Lord, who performed much violence with firearms every week in his usual time slot. Mr. Lord felt that "all guns should be taken away from the citizens of the country and given only to law enforcement officers and armed service members. The statement by sportsmen that they should have guns to kill poor innocent deer to control them is a lot of bull. I don't go for it. I've seen some gun lovers with dozens of weapons in their homes. Why? They wouldn't be able to use them against robbers; they would be too panicky. Something should be done about outlawing guns."

Especially in the hands of actors!

Cleaning out the garage was a favorite pastime during the 1970s. Wives were forever urging their reluctant spouses to lighten the load by casting overboard some treasured possession. No telling how many stuffed mooseheads from

Uncle Herman got unceremoniously exiled to the land fill. Then cartoonist Chuck Asay decided to tweak the noses of the gun control crowd with a wonderful two-frame cartoon that just fit perfectly with their view of the world.

Here's the first frame:

Here's the second frame:

Not quite what the gun grabbers had in mind.

Case #2

Anti-gun Surgeon General Joycelyn Elders

Can you imagine being a high ranking federal official who gets headlines for extreme anti-gun rhetoric—and having a son who gets arrested for being a drug pusher?

Welcome to the world of former Surgeon General Joycelyn Elders. In 1993, after her confirmation as the nation's Top Doc, she went before a congressional hearing and called death by gunfire an epidemic ravaging American society, and urged parents to fight it by refusing to give children toy guns.

"Please think twice before buying that toy gun for a child. These toy guns are not child's play," she told Congress.

Here we go again, this time with two really dumb arguments.

First, Dr. Elders forgot everything she learned in those years in medical school about epidemiology by treating handgun violence as a medical epidemic. It's not.

There is no medical cause of people misusing guns to commit crimes. There is no germ or genetic flaw or allergic reaction that makes people reach for a handgun to shoot someone. Disease doesn't make you use guns. Hurting people, with guns or anything else, is an act of volition. You have to do it on purpose.

Second, toy guns *are* most certainly child's play. Think of all the generations of kids that have grown up into responsible adults playing with toy guns.

True, not all of them went on to become great generals or law enforcement officers or career enlisted military—but how are we to instill the courage and resourcefulness required for our armed defenders if we stop kids from playing with guns?

And what about the simple guts to defend yourself in a pinch? Are we trying to raise a generation of hapless victims and huddled masses forever waiting for the cops to come?

Playing with guns as a kid helps to develop a strong sense of self—and parents who instill respect for guns and provide firearms training are creating competent and responsible future adults.

What's a smart doctor like Joycelyn Elders up to using the dumbest anti-gun arguments? It was beneath her dignity as the nation's Top Doc.

All this worry about crime had a hollow ring coming from Dr. Elders because of her own family situation. Her 29-year-old son Kevin was convicted in July 1994 of selling an eighth of an ounce of cocaine to a police informant in 1993. He was sentenced to 10 years in prison, but was freed on a bond pending appeal.

In June, 1995 the Arkansas Supreme Court affirmed the drug conviction. In a unanimous ruling, the Supreme Court said Kevin Elders did not prove he was entrapped. The defendant contended that he was forced to sell cocaine to a friend and police informant who he said threatened to publicize his drug addiction on the eve of his mother's confirmation hearing. The informant, Calvin Walraven, committed suicide after the trial.

Perhaps a lecture to Congress about the epidemic of drug abuse in this country would have been more apt.

In fact, at that same congressional hearing, Curtis Sliwa, leader of New York City's crime-fighting Guardian Angels, said that "dope-sucking psychopaths" were the real problem in gun crime. He ought to know—he sustained a near-fatal wounding by a still-unidentified gunman in 1992. He believes the assailant was on drugs.

If police are going to crack down on anyone, it should be the druggies and peddlers that pollute the minds and lives of our youngsters.

World Class Dumb-Downs

The Media

You know what they say about network television: It's nationwide—and half an inch deep.

The rest of the media aren't a whole lot better. Newspapers, magazines.

When it comes to guns, the media are the champion dumb-downers.

You want dumb about guns, look at the media. The media's anti-gun bias is so stupid you wonder why they can't see it themselves.

If it's about guns, reporters, news anchors, editorial boards—the whole works—just assume it's bad.

If you want to see how obvious the problem really is, just think back to the visit by a Japanese dignitary who said to the media, "American workers are lazy."

That got the adrenaline pumping, as the perceptive Chuck Asay cartoon shows below. But if the subject were to turn to guns, and a foreign visitor were to make a similarly inflammatory remark, the media would....

Would what?

You guess.

Then turn the page to see what cartoonist Chuck Asay thought.

ADVICE TO FOREIGNERS WHO WISH TO SAY ANYTHING CRITICAL ABOUT AMERICANS: ALWAYS PICK TOPICS IN WHICH YOU AND THE AMERICAN MEDIA AGREE!

You guessed it.

Are the media fair?
I always say yes, they're fair.
They misquote everybody equally.

But are they also biased?
You can get an idea from the list of media
I've compiled based on their publication
of consistently anti-gun editorials and
feature stories. These are just the
biggest culprits. There's a lot of anti-
gun bias in more local media, too.

World Class Anti-gun Media

ABC - American Broadcasting Company

NBC - National Broadcasting Company

CBS - Columbia Broadcasting System

Cosmopolitan

New England Journal of Medicine

Boston Globe

Life Magazine

Family Circle

Ms Magazine

People Magazine

Ann Landers (columnist)

Marianne Means (columnist)

Parade Magazine

Washington Post

Newsday

The New York Times

Time Magazine

World Class Anti-gun Media

Newsweek, Inc.

Chicago Tribune

USA Today

San Jose Mercury News

The Los Angeles Times

Miami Herald

The Baltimore Sun

McCall's Magazine

MTV

Rolling Stone

Glamour Magazine

Turner Broadcasting

That's a short list Hall of Shame. These media outlets are so rabidly anti-gun they don't even make a pretense of objectivity.

If you recall about New York Times publisher Arthur Ochs "Punch" Sulzberger, he has a concealed carry gun permit, one of the few in the Big Apple. He just doesn't want you to have one, that's all.

Kid's Stuff

Did that remark of Dr. Joycelyn Elders about toy guns not being child's play get to you?

I think it got to Charles Memminger, a columnist for the Honolulu (Hawaii) Star-Bulletin. He wrote a column about cowboys, Ninjas and toy guns. Here's how he opened:

"Am I the only one who's noticed that you can't buy a decent toy gun anymore?

"I was in a large toy store recently looking for a cowboy outfit for my daughter. OK, cowgirl outfit. Whatever. We're talking basically about a hat, simulated buckskin vest and a double holster with a pair of six shooters. I knew exactly the kind I wanted, the same kind I had when I was a kid: real leather holster with heavy-duty cap guns that you could twirl on you finger like Palladin."

Did our intrepid columnist find what he was looking for ?

"No such luck. They had plastic Ninja swords for you to conk your friend on the head with. They had various Nerf rocket gizmos for you to shoot your friends in the face with. They had all manner of heavy bats and batons for you to beat the hell out of your neighbor with. But I couldn't find any cowboy outfits."

No cowboy stuff at all?

"Hey, where are the guns?" the columnist asked.

Reasonable question in a toy store, right?

Wrong.

The clerk looked at the columnist "like I was an adjutant general in the Michigan Militia.

"We don't sell guns," she said in a voice dripping with righteous indignation.

"Look, I don't mean real guns," the columnist said. "I mean cowboy cap guns. Where are they?"

"We don't sell cowboy guns of any sort," she snorted.

"What kind of cowboy stuff do you have?" he asked.

She showed him a little felt-type hat that looked more like a Howdy-Doody topper than a real cowboy hat.

"That's not a cowboy hat," the columnist said. "That's some kind of derby or something. How's a kid supposed to play cowboy without any cowboy stuff?"

The clerk made it clear that playing cowboy was simply not done these days. Instead she directed the columnist toward a leatherette Indian maiden outfit. It's all right for kids to play Indian maidens, mainly because Disney says so. Indian maidens were sensitive to the environment. Cowboys walked in the house with cow stuff on their boots. Indian maidens ate wild hickory nuts. Cowboys had buffalo breath.

"Let me get this straight," said the columnist. "You don't sell any toy gun. But you do sell this ninja outfit complete with a long sword for conking your friends with and a short plastic dagger and a plastic throwing death star?"

The clerk conceded that was about the size of it.

Frankly, the columnist said, I don't get it.

"We had great times as kids dressing up like cowboys. We would stage gunfights on the lawn. The idea was to see who could die the best. We used to argue about whose turn it was to die. My buddy Tommy was an expert at dying. Sometimes, it would take Tommy half the morning to die. We'd draw and fire, he'd go down and start writhing around on the ground saying things like, "You got me, pilgrim. I'm a-dyin.'"

"I'd go inside and have some milk and cookies and come out a while later and he'd still be in his death throes. ("It's a gettin' dark, partner. I'm a-headin' down the trail.")

"I don't see anything particularly wrong with a couple of kids pretending like they are engaged in an honorable and dignified fight to the death. It's not like we practiced shooting each other from moving cars."

Well, the columnist realized sadly, cowboys are out and ninjas are in.

Toy six-shooters are bad. Swords are good.

"I don't get it," he repeated plaintively.

"Weren't ninjas paid assassins, who used to sneak into people's houses while they slept and cut their throats?" he asked.

"That's a great thing to teach kids," he grumped.

"I can just imagine Tommy and me on a Saturday morning.

"Okay, Tommy, you be the poor guy fast asleep and I'll be the guy who sneaks in and cuts your throat."

"Then I'd climb through the window, pounce on the bed and drag the plastic dagger across his gullet. Then Tommy'd start writhing around going, "I'm a-dyin,' pilgrim-san."

"And I'd say, "No, Tommy, I'm a trained assassin, you die in your sleep. There's no talkin' or anything."

And he'd say, "I'm going to play at Cindy's house. At least we get to wrestle with a tomahawk and eat wild hickory nuts."

"Do you have a permit for that banana?"

"Family Circus" cartoonist Bil Keane brings his usual gentle humor to the gun control issue.

World Class Dumb-Downs

Misplaced Priorities

Gun bans.
Stupid.
Waiting periods.
Stupid.
Blame the gun.
Stupid.
Gun amnesty.
Stupid.
Stop toy guns.
Stupid.

When will we get smart?

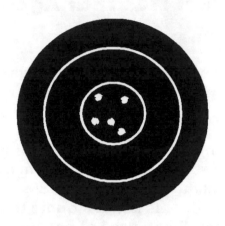

Part Three

How to
Shoot Yourself in the Foot

Alan's Dictionary: **shoot•yourself•in•the•foot**
v 1 : metatarsal puncture wound sustained when an over-eager and under-bright gunfighter pulls the trigger before he or she draws.
2 : *figurative* : result of failing to make sure brain is loaded before shooting off mouth.
3 : *political colloquial* : making a policy that back-fires by hurting the innocent while having no effect on the guilty—what the gun control crowd does every time they try to play doctor with your Second Amendment rights.

What Was That Again?

The law enforcement executive of the Balti-more County Police Department, Leonard Supenski, is widely known as a strident anti-gun advocate.

During the early 1990s, he supposedly did a look-back study of law enforcement officers killed in the line of duty during the 1980s.

He made this famous quote to the Los Angeles Times: "We're tired of passing out flags to the widows of officers killed by drug dealers with Uzis."

Concerned, *The New Gun Week* news staff queried the FBI about Supenski's statement.

J. Harper Wilson, Chief of the FBI's Uniform Crime Reporting Program reviewed his database and found there was only one such incident in the entire 1980-1989 period, and it was nowhere near Baltimore County.

"One Puerto Rico police officer was shot and killed on October 13, 1981, by a subject who was intoxicated with marijuana and armed with a semi-automatic 9mm Model A Uzi. This was the only listing for a law enforcement officer killed with an Uzi."

Wilson also stated "there were 828 officers feloniously killed in the line of duty from 1980 through 1989. Sixty-six were killed in drug-related matters but not necessarily by drug dealers and could have been killed by drug users who were high or intoxicated at the time of the killing."

No Cover Charge - Or Else

The Drug Enforcement Administration is a serious federal agency. DEA Agents are serious people.

You better take them seriously, or they might shoot you, even if you're the operator of a topless bar that merely asks for a five buck cover charge to see the uncovered ladies.

That's what happened in mid-1995 when Pete Sinclair, a DEA agent, threw a bachelor party for himself at the classy Ritz Cabaret, a Houston, Texas topless nightclub.

Things turned violent when Sinclair didn't like the bar manager's demands for a $5 cover charge for his guests.

So the DEA agent shot the owner, Stavros Fotinopoulos, who took 5 bullets from Sinclair's 9mm pistol. Y'all don't mess with the DEA, y'hear?

Fotinopoulos shot back, giving Sinclair two bullet wounds. Sinclair was hospitalized in fair condition, Fotinopoulos in poor condition.

Sinclair, 28, fired first, said Donald Ferrarone, DEA agent in charge in Houston. The agent's gun was missing.

The DEA didn't report what Sinclair's bride-to-be had to say about all this.

Attack of the Killer Donuts

Drive-By Donut Strafing
Nets Two Suspects

In 1994, Middleford, Maine, police arrested two men for a drive-by donut attack , according to Reuters news syndicate.

The two were charged with assault. They admitted to pelting a pedestrian with pastries from a passing car. A third man was being sought.

The victim, Laurie Remillard, told police she was walking when she was hit in the face by a salvo of donut holes sprayed from a passing vehicle. Ms. Remillard recorded the car's license plate when it returned for a second assault.

Police said the suspects, Chris Roy, 19, and Christopher Cote, 20, admitted they were not strangers to throwing donuts, but said they normally target street signs and are not sure why they turned on a human victim.

There are no donut control laws in America. No wonder donut nuts are running around armed to the teeth.

You don't see reports like this coming from Britain.

Demon Gun

Cleric Urges Parishioners
to Drive Out Guns

Rev. Marshall Gourley of Our Lady of Guadalupe Church in Denver, Colorado, said in a sermon a few years ago that "guns are demons."

He implored his flock to turn in their guns. His congregation was not too sure of the theology behind this call. One person even suggested that the Rev. Gourley could stand a little education.

"One thing pro-gunners in the parish could do," he suggested, "is when the collection basket comes around, put spent cartridge shells in it instead of the customary monetary offering."

Pro-gun lobbyist John Snyder suggested that St. Gabriel Posenti be designated Patron of Handgunners by the Sacred Congregation for the Causes of Saints in Rome. St. Gabriel is the 19th Century Italian handgun marksman who rescued the inhabitants of Isola, Italy, from a band of marauders with a courageous demonstration of handgun marksmanship.

Warren Burger's Guns

When former Chief Justice Warren Burger died in June of 1995, not many people remembered his views on guns as being anything but an anti-gun stand in the United States Supreme Court.

He was best known for his 1990 support of stricter regulation of gun owners and would-be gun buyers to "put a stop to mindless homicidal carnage."

But did the public know that the Chief Justice had owned sporting guns all his life when he sided with the gun control crowd on the high court?

And did the public remember that in 1979, Burger's ownership of a pistol made news when the armed Chief Justice confronted a newspaper reporter who had gone to Burger's home late one night seeking comment on a story?

Rock Control - Ban the Stones

The problem of rocks being thrown at cars off highway bypasses in Delaware became serious when several motorists were injured by the stones.

A letter-writer sent advice to a newspaper, "Just get Sen. Joseph Biden to outlaw rocks. Surely if it will work to lower gun crime, it should work for the bypass."

The noted anti-gun advocate, then-chairman of the Senate Judiciary Committee, did not respond.

Warren Burger's Guns, Part 2

After retiring from the bench, former Chief Justice Warren Burger made some anti-gun claims about the Second Amendment. He insisted that it simply guarantees the people the right to serve in the national guard—because of the clause that a militia is necessary to the security of a free state.

Mike McCabe, an attorney for the NRA, was appalled by Burger's historical blindness, and offered a few lessons in constitutional history and what the Founding Fathers actually meant.

He noted that the New Hampshire convention proposed that, "Congress shall never disarm any citizen, unless such as are or have been in actual rebellion." It lists no purpose for possessing arms.

He also cited the Pennsylvania minority proposal, "that the people have a right to bear arms for defense of themselves and their own State, or the United States, or for the purpose of killing game; and no law shall be passed for disarming the people or any of them, unless for crimes committed, or real danger of public injury from individuals; and as standing armies in time of peace are dangerous to liberty, they ought not to be kept up; and the military shall be kept under strict subordination to and governed by the civil power."

That somewhat verbose proposal covered all traditional purposes for possessing arms.

It also made it rather clear that the present Second Amendment has two distinct purposes: one to establish a militia; the other to guarantee an individual right to own and use guns. Mr. Burger did not respond.

Gee Whiz Award

To Columnist Mike Royko

For finally waking up, nationally syndicated newspaper columnist Mike Royko gets the
Late Bloomer Gun Appreciation Prize of $1.

After many years as a leading anti-gun po-
lemicist, Mike Royko wrote a 1993 column indicating a shift in awareness.

"I probably wrote more columns on the
issue of the availability of handguns than any
columnist in the United States," Royko said.

"Finally, I noticed something else. Strict
gun laws are about as effective as strict drug
laws. The drugs flow and so does the supply of
weapons. It pains me to say this, but the NRA
seems to be right: The cities and states that have
the toughest gun laws have the most murder and

mayhem. Just as junkies find drugs, criminals find weapons. And I haven't the faintest idea how to prevent it.

"And now we've reached the point where most law-abiding gun owners believe that they need their guns because of all the artillery that is in the hands of the loonies. They are against unilateral disarmament."

Gun Control at Work

Here's an educational case:

On August 12, 1994, Mrs. Polly S. Przybyl, 36, a federally licensed gun dealer and mother of two, left her husband of 17 years, Lee S. Przybyl, 40.

Two days later, she and her two children found it necessary to hide from her estranged husband at her mother's home in Cheektowaga, New York, just north of Buffalo.

Mr. Przybyl followed her and tried to get in, so Mrs. Przybyl called police.

"When police arrived, Mrs. Przybyl was waving a gun in the presence of children, and we took it away from her," said Cheektowaga police Lt. Cheryl Rucinski, adding that police confiscated a second handgun belonging to her.

Seven days after losing her handguns, Mrs. Przybyl and her mother, Gloria C. Mason, drove to the wife's former home to pick up clothing belonging to the children.

Mr. Przybyl shot the two women to death outside the family home. Mrs. Przybyl was shot two times in the head and stabbed in the heart. Her mother was shot twice in the abdomen. Eleven hours later, Mr. Przybyl used one of his shotguns to kill himself.

Rita Smith, Coordinator of the Denver-based National Coalition Against Domestic Violence, said many women threatened by abusive men believe owning a gun is their "only option" because "police protection is spotty and discretionary."

Gray Kleck, Professor of Criminology and Criminal Justice at Florida State University, said, "It's appalling that the police didn't make a distinction between the aggressor and the victim. They shouldn't have taken the gun away from the wife, who was the clear victim. And given the fact that she had a legal permit, I don't know if they had legal grounds."

Kids! Be a Cartoon Character!

Say Something Bad About Guns And We'll Make You A Screen Star

Alliance Communications of Toronto organized a neato anti-gun drive, kids! You can now trade in your toy guns for a chance to become a Saturday morning cartoon character on television!

ReBoot, a television cartoon program broadcast on the ABC Television Network Saturday mornings, asked children in early 1995 to send in a toy gun with a letter or drawing explaining why it is wrong to play with violent toys.

The winner got the chance to have a computer-generated character created of themselves in the television program for the 1966 season.

Steven DeNure, president of production at Alliance Communications, said, "We created this promotion called 'Non-Violence Builds Character' to teach kids that guns, even toy guns, are dangerous."

The television program was produced by using computer generated imagery and 3D animation. ReBoot follows three main characters living in an electronic world controlled by an unseen character inside the central processing unit of a personal computer.

The Wizard of Id makes a gun control point.

Pull, Jane, Pull!

This is Jane. See Jane talk. See Jane talk in the movies. See Jane in Hanoi aiming an anti-aircraft gun to shoot down American planes. See Americans boo Jane.

See Hanoi Jane grow older. See Jane marry Ted Turner. See Ted run his CNN cable news network. Run, Ted, run! See Ted and Jane at all the politically correct social functions. See Ted and Jane say nasty things about guns. See Ted and Jane speak out for gun control.

See Ted and Jane sign up to take wing-shooting lessons at the Orvis School in northern Florida. They learn to shoot clay pigeons, not live ones. Bang, bang, bang!

See Ted and Jane use shotguns in the sport. Hear Ted and Jane shout "Pull!" See a clay pigeon get released. See them shoot, shoot, shoot!

See Ted and Jane keep this a secret from their politically correct friends. Hmm....

Celebrities With Anti-Gun Pull

Here's the short list of anti-gun celebrities you may have heard of.

Jane Fonda - Actor
Steve Allen - Entertainer
Ed Asner - Actor
Lauren Bacall - Actor
Candice Bergen - Actress
Robert E. Brennan - Financier
Jimmy Breslin - Columnist
Beau Bridges - Actor
Lloyd Bridges - Actor
Dr. Joyce Brothers - Psychologist-Author
Art Buchwald - Columnist
Robert Chartloff - Producer
Julia Child - Author - TV Chef
Pam Dawber - Actor
Amitai Etzioni - Professor
Mike Farrell - Actor
Art Garfunkel - Singer
James Glassman - Editor
Louis Gossett, Jr. - Actor
Bryant Gumbel - Entertainer
Mariette Hartley - Actor
Hal Holbrook - Actor
Maynard Jackson - former Atlanta Mayor
C. Everett Koop - former Surgeon General
William Kovacs - Director
Ann Landers - Columnist
Norman Lear - Producer, Activist
Jack Lemmon - Actor
Hal Linden - Actor
That's a lot of pull!

Let's See If I've Got This Right

About That Guy Who Shot At
The White House

This squib appeared in the National Review
*shortly after a lone gunman fired a semiautomatic
weapon at the White House from a public street:*

Assault rifles were banned by the Clinton
Crime Bill in 1994.
The Crime Bill passed!
Even Republicans voted for it!
It was signed into law!
Assault weapons are illegal.
You cannot have one.
Nobody has one.
They are all gone.
They will never bother the decent citizens of
this country again.
Crime has ended.
We outlawed crime.
Nobody would have shot at the White House
with an assault weapon.
Clinton flacks must have made up the whole
incident.

Thanks for that nice bit of parody, *National Review.*

Of course, it wasn't an "assault rifle," but a Chinese semiautomatic.

That's okay.

Most of the people who supported the Crime Bill didn't know the difference either.

Ohio City's Gun Buyback

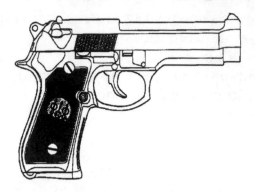

A "Feel-Good" Event
With No Redeeming Virtues

B. Frank Jacoby, co-editor of a newsletter for the pro-gun group, Peoples Rights Organization, wrote a guest column for the *Columbus Dispatch* about the city's gun buyback program.

"The great Columbus gun buyback is over," Jacoby wrote, "and it was a splendid 'feel-good' success for the news media and city leaders. There were wonderful pictures of boxes of guns being hauled 'off the street' and heart-warming stories of widows turning in their husband's old guns to buy groceries. Finally, something was being done about 'gun violence' ... or was it?

"Let's understand the essence of this program. It's a fact more people are killed by motor vehicles than guns, but if the city launched a buyback program to get cars 'off the streets, no questions asked,' it would be derided as the dumbest idea of the century.

"But change the focus to something as scary as guns, and suddenly everyone ignores the real-ity of market forces.

"What happens with any such ill-advised program is that you end up with the biggest collection of junkers the world has ever seen. While there certainly is some value in getting junk firearms 'off the street,' one has to ask whether it is worth the price.

"The question becomes even more important when you realize that the anonymous nature of a handgun turn-in program induces every punk in town to think about stealing a gun to make a quick $75.

"If he just happened to stick up a carry-out and shoot the clerk with it on the way to turn it in, the city will be happy to destroy a key piece of evidence and pay the perpetrator.

"One even has to wonder whether the buyback induced senior citizens to turn in antique firearms for a fraction of their real value."

The Naked Truth About Crime

Armed Minister   Disrobes Burglar

The Reverend Ronald Kirk, armed with a pistol, responded to a security alarm about 11:30 a.m. on April 29, 1994. He discovered two men removing stuff from his church, according to a report in the *Buffalo News*.

One of the two escaped, but Kirk was able to detain the other at gunpoint.

He was alone. How could he immobilize the suspect and be sure he was unarmed while he phoned police?

Kirk ordered the man to strip naked. The man obeyed.

While Kirk called police, the man escaped out into the street.

However, he was not too difficult to spot among passersby. Buffalo, New York, is not a big nudist spot.

The suspect was taken into custody and charged.

Double Standards, Anyone?

Another buyback item:

There was this guy named Fernando Mateo. He's a New York City rug merchant. He spearheaded the "Toys for Guns Bonus Amnesty" in the Big Apple.

Big hero. The media fell all over themselves covering him with glory.

However, *The Orange County Register*, a California newspaper, came up with a little item.

It seems that Mr. Mateo himself is above all that. He refused to turn in his own .38-caliber revolver in exchange for concert tickets, toys or hamburgers.

Mateo has not only owned the gun for over 10 years, but also has actually used it at least once to scare off some thugs in his store.

Very practical man, Mateo.

Anti-Gun Advocate Thinks Twice

To Shoot or Not To Shoot

Anti-gun newspaper columnist Jodine Mayberry found herself one day in 1992 in a place she always thought she would never be, doing something she was positive she would never do. Here's what she wrote in the *Delaware County Daily Times*:

"I was standing in a booth at Dusty Rhoads' firing range in Marcus Hooks, Pennsylvania, firing a handgun at a drawing of an assailant pinned up 10 feet away. I wasn't doing half bad."

"Since I am a card-carrying member of Handgun Control, Inc., do not own a gun myself and never expect to, it came as a great surprise to me that I had agreed to this outing and that I was actually enjoying myself.

"This all started when my friend Carol called me one day and asked me if she should buy a gun.

"Carol had just gotten out of a brutal four-year marriage, one that was marked by bruises, black eyes, hours spent in hospital emergency rooms, frantic calls to the police and at least two protection-from-abuse orders."

"Carol's ex-husband was in prison at the time, but he would get out—and probably look up his former wife to brutalize, and perhaps kill.

"So when she asked me if I thought she should buy a gun, what would I say? 'Don't worry about it?'

"Yeah," I said, "If it will make you feel safer, get a gun."

"So the two of us went to a local gun shop where she purchased a .25-caliber automatic that cost $100. Admittedly, it isn't much of a gun. A .38-caliber revolver would have been better, but it was all that Carol could afford.

"The gun dealer told her she should go to a firing range and learn how to use the gun.

"This is just plain good sense. If you're going to own a gun, you ought to know how to use it, which is why I went on down to Dusty Rhoads.

"Give me a target with a crotch," Carol said, making the men in the store laugh nervously. "It'll inspire me."

"So how do I feel about all this, avid (some would say rabid) gun control freak that I am?

"I don't know. I know that the vast majority of gun owners never hurt anyone and that they derive a great deal of pleasure out of using their guns for lawful purposes, target shooting, hunting, protection and collecting.

"Carol? She sleeps much better now that she has her gun close at hand. My hope is that she never has to use it.

"Still, if she ever does have to use it to protect herself against her violent ex-husband, I hope she doesn't miss."

A Potato WHAT?

A Potato *Gun*, Stupid!

Okay, I've been from here to there in this galaxy. Seen a lot of strange stuff. But I never saw a potato gun.

What, you reasonably ask, is a potato gun?

Let me quote from an authoritative source, *The New Gun Week* of Friday, July 8, 1994:

"The potato gun generally consists of a length of pipe wired to an igniter. The potato or other projectile is propelled by a blast of propane."

So you see, it's not *really* what you think of as a *gun*.

But Crystal Lake, Illinois, police think it is. Police Chief Keith Nygren's officer had confiscated potato guns from two carloads of youths, according to a *Chicago Sun-Times* story, and he said he fears more may be in circulation because a segment on MTV showed college kids firing such weapons.

"If we came across two of them, you can imagine there are a whole lot more of them out there. Our concern is we want parents and people who might pick up one of these things to realize just how dangerous they are," Nygren said.

The teenagers who had the potato guns were not using them against people, but were simply shooting them out in isolated areas to see how far the potatoes would travel. The fact that they went up to 200 yards indicates how powerful these devices are, Nygren said.

"It really hasn't dawned on these kids how dangerous these things are," he said. "Depending on how solid the gas chamber is, it could explode when you ignite it, sending shrapnel into your body or that of anyone else standing nearby. It presents a hazard to the user and whoever this thing is shot at.

"The velocity of whatever you stick down the barrel is extremely high."

Nygren warned that someone hit by a potato from such a gun fired at short range could be killed.

Well, you learn something new every day, if you don't watch it.

Now is Chief Nygren trying to enforce gun control?

Or is that potato control?

Hmm?

Get the Facts, ABC News

At Least Get the Words Right

When the "assault weapon" ban was before Congress in 1994, an edition of *This Week With David Brinkley* featured newsman Sam Donaldson discussing the issue.

You guessed it, Sam didn't like "assault weapons" and wanted to ban them.

He wasn't quite clear what an assault rifle was, however. He stumbled and bumbled about semiautomatic firearms and fully automatic firearms and generally conveyed his feeling that whatever assault weapons were, he was sure they were bad.

Poor guy. I felt like prompting him with a few facts and definitions. But then I saw Sam do something really dumb. Others caught it too—I know, because I ran across a letter to Sam from Dave Smith of Elma, Washington, commenting on the very thing that bothered me.

Here are a few choice excerpts:

Dear Mr. Donaldson:

A few weeks ago on *This Week With David Brinkley*, you were discussing the "assault rifle" issue with David Brinkley. You were pontificating on the tremendous evil of these guns, when he asked "Isn't it true that most firearms crimes are committed with handguns?" You answered to the effect, "Well, I'm really not sure."

Mr. Donaldson, given the intensity with which you argue this topic, don't you think you should have a little more knowledge of the subject? Say, for example, looking at the FBI statistics? David was right. "Assault" firearms figure in only a small percentage of crimes nationwide.

I have no intention of trying to sway your views, because even if you did believe differently, you couldn't express your views because your employers and colleagues would quickly make it clear that you must be Politically Correct.

However, you could at least take the time to get the nuts and bolts information straight.

Try not to be like Jane Fonda in the 'Sixties, who, in a rare moment of candor, stated that she made it a point not to read anything that opposed her viewpoints, because she feared that conflicting information might weaken her resolve.

Good advice for ABC News, Dave.

Good Shot

Hot Pants for Thug

The young man's story didn't wash with the doctors at Fairview Riverside Medical Center in Minneapolis.

The 25-year-old man had told them how an altercation in north Minneapolis had left a .22-caliber bullet in his buttocks.

There was one little problem: The pants he arrived in didn't have a bullet hole. As in all gunshot wounds, doctors called the police.

Police had already issued a bulletin about the attempted robbery in St. Paul of Jermaine Givens, 16. Givens told investigators that three intruders wearing ski masks had kicked in the door of his mother's home, demanded money and led them outside.

Givens was shot in the leg but then wrestled a gun from one assailant and shot him in the buttocks as he fled. Givens was treated at St. Paul-Ramsey Medical Center for his wound and released.

The 25-year-old suspect was arrested at the hospital and listed in fair condition after being booked on suspicion of aggravated robbery, assault and burglary.

Police were searching in St. Paul for pants with a bullet hole.

Oh, yes, and for the two other men and a blue Oldsmobile Cutlass.

Hey, You Forgot
To Turn In Your Gun

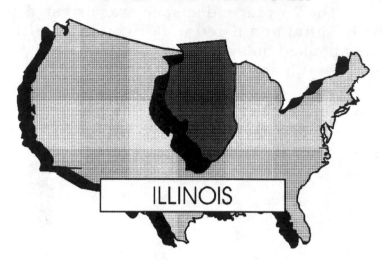

ILLINOIS

Candidate Makes Little Small Mistake

Illinois Attorney General Roland Burris was a major promoter of the 1993 Gun Turn-In Day in Chicago.

He was also a candidate for nomination as Governor of Illinois in 1994.

Then the *Chicago Tribune* caught him with his handgun still at home.

The *Trib* ran a story noting that while Attorney General Burris persuaded others to turn in their guns, he had somehow failed to persuade himself to do likewise.

When asked why he didn't turn in his own gun, Burris told members of the *Tribune*'s editorial board:

"I just didn't get around to doing it."

"It's a little, small thing," Burris said—presumably talking about his gun size, not his brain size.

"I just have it there for safety. If I ban them, I'm going to be the first one to burn mine."

Run that statement through your mind again, and see if it doesn't smell like something familiar.

He just has it there for safety.

A trifling reason that voters should ignore.

And he's going to *burn* his gun?

Well, yes, gun steel will burn, but you're talking a few thousand degrees Fahrenheit.

Like a blast furnace.

Oh, well.

Burris still had his gun, but the story generated enough heat about his hypocrisy that a few days later he surrendered his own gun.

Did the voters give him a gun amnesty?

Well, does this tell you anything?

When the election was over, the Governor's name wasn't Roland Burris (It was Jim Edgar).

Now this probably doesn't mean anything, but if you go into the State of Illinois Home Page on the World Wide Web, you won't even find the Attorney General's Office mentioned among the State Agencies.

A mere oversight, no doubt.

Congress As Gun Runner

How to Make a Run on Guns

So Congress wants to enforce gun control.

The House passes the Brady Bill, which requires a mandatory waiting period and background checks for all gun purchases.

So what do people do?

Of course.

They rush out and buy a gun before the law goes into effect.

A gun dealer near Washington, D.C. on the Virginia side of the Potomac sold half a dozen guns the day after Congress passed the Brady Bill—before he even opened for business.

People called overnight and gave him their credit card numbers over the phone. He sold 13 assault-style rifles before noon.

The gun controllers caused a run on guns.

A gun dealer in nearby Silver Spring, Maryland, said he'd seen a lot of first-time buyers who felt that if they were ever going to buy a gun, now was the time to do it, before Congress stops it.

That's the best way to get people to buy guns I can think of—make it known that you're going to ban them.

It's almost as good as the city ordinance passed by Kennesaw, Georgia, requiring every homeowner to possess a weapon for self defense (conscientious objectors excused).

Sort of the opposite of Morton Grove, Illinois, which passed a village ordinance prohibiting the ownership of handguns.

Guess which one has more crooks hanging out there?

The Benson cartoon below says it all.

Don't Leave Home Without It

No Guns for Paranoids

I was researching my *Celebrity Address Book* in the Rolls Royce of Zoltar, a millionaire Hollywood producer, when he showed me his .45-caliber semiautomatic on the way to the set.

"I keep Teddy right here on the seat," he said proudly. "We can't be too careful these days."

"That's great," I said, "but I thought the movie you're producing has an anti-gun message."

"*Raving Lunatics*? It does! It's about a bunch of right-wing wackos who start defending themselves from criminals in this little Iowa town and end up arming the whole nation."

"But, Zoltar, if you have a gun to protect yourself from criminals, how can you make an anti-gun film about people who do the same thing?"

"Hey, Alan, baby, you don't understand. These guys in my film are heavy duty right-wingers. Paranoids. They think people are out to get them. Say, did you notice that guy in the blue Olsdmobile that keeps looking at my Rolls in his mirror?"

"No, where?"

"Passed us about ten minutes ago. Now, these right-wingers start out criticizing the government for not protecting them. We set up the scene perfectly. Somebody kills one of them and the heavy takes it personal-like. Hey, look at those guys in the baseball caps over in the oncoming lanes. They're laughing at me. Teddy would like nothing better than to let loose with a warning shot across the hood ornament."

"Are you that good a shot?"

"You bet, baby. I was personally given instruction by Jane Fonda herself. Now, the wackos in my movie aren't like us. They're nobodies. No Rolls Royce. No nice homes in Beverly Hills. Riff-raff. They'll never eat lunch in this town. You know the type, Alan."

"I *am* the type, Zoltar. But how does your movie end?"

"We're working on that right now. The whole country starts arming itself. Our screen writers are having trouble with a good ending."

"Really? Why?"

"All our characters get real polite because *everybody* carries a gun. We can't work out a hot ending with lots of explosions. Its too peaceful. Hey, look at those kids at the studio gate."

"They're just waving, Zoltar."

"They're going to grow up to be right-wing paranoids. We've got to keep guns away from paranoids. That's the message of my movie, Alan. The paranoids are out to get us."

"Thanks for the ride, Zoltar."

"And you watch for *Raving Lunatics*, Alan."

Aussies Abandon Gun Registry

In 1983, the Australian state of Victoria introduced a system of universal firearms registration. In 1995, Victoria's Minister of Police, equivalent to a U.S. state attorney general or Canadian provincial solicitor-general, had to admit the 12-year exercise had been a waste of time.

At an annual meeting, police ministers of Australia's eight states conceded that there had not been a single incident in the entire country in which gun registration had prevented a crime or helped solve one.

The eight ministers decided to abandon the universal registration schemes they were implementing or considering, and to administer instead a national system of gun owner licensing. It would appear the citizens of Victoria gave up on the mandatory registration scheme much earlier, however; The Victoria minister of police admitted that more than 73% of the guns in the state were still unregistered after 12 years.

Goofy Gun Laws

News flash! Did you know that in Pickens, Oklahoma, it's strictly a violation of the law for a woman over 200 pounds and attired in shorts to carry a gun while riding a horse in public?

On to South Carolina: Church-going family men are required by state law to "carry two loaded horse pistols, in good working order" when taking the family to church or to any church-related activities. That's to keep the men from carrying old rusty inoperable horse pistols, which would be unsightly.

Now up in Michigan: Maple Ridge forbids women to hold a gun in their lap and read the Sunday paper while sitting in a rocking chair on their front porch. Was it the newspaper companies or the rocking chair manufacturers who lobbied for that one?

Old Furnace, Massachusetts, has a law against whistling while carrying a gun over your shoulder on Sunday. Massachusetts has always had anti-music legislators.

Florida: Women can't shoot the hats from the heads of other women citizens while walking down the street. Let's see if we can figure out why *that* law was passed. No, let's don't.

Well, it sounds fair: In Mississippi's common law, "Every citizen has the right to shoot to kill if necessary when escorting a woman home from a quilting party and another man interferes and threatens to shoot him." Those quilting parties can get pretty wild, you know.

Cascade, Iowa: It's illegal to duel with water pistols. A conservation law, no doubt.

A law for sissies: If you're a woman in Pattonsburg, Missouri, you can be arrested if you make "silly or insulting faces" at a man while he's practicing his shooting skills. The guys in that town must need the practice.

They're much more reasonable in Wakefield, Rhode Island. There, a woman may not fire in the direction of a policeman with intent to shoot off his necktie. Just plain common sense, if you ask me.

But you have to go to Texas for a truly rational approach to crime. Not long ago, Texas passed what is known as its anti-crime law. The statute requires a criminal to give the intended victim twenty-four hours' notice, either orally or in writing. The victim must be properly notified of the nature of the crime to be committed and the time and place at which it will happen. Criminals, I assume, need not R.S.V.P. their victims. That's just too, too cute.

In Spades, Indiana, you aren't allowed to open a can of food by shooting at it with a revolver. The law is silent on whether you may use a rifle or machine gun.

All you graduates of the Jedi Academy, tell Yoda and Luke Skywalker not to visit North Andover, Massachusetts, where a local law prohibits citizens from carrying "space guns." Leave your blaster home—but I wonder if you can carry your light saber....

Be a man, use a gun! Truro, Mississippi,

requires a young suitor to "prove himself manly" to both prospective bride and future father-in-law. The hopeful swain must proceed to the woods and there shoot six blackbirds—or three crows if blackbirds prove uncooperative. The dead birds must then be presented to the prospective father-in-law as proof of the young man's masculinity. Do you think a law like this in New York City would require you to bag six muggers, for which you could substitute three bank robbers?

None of this namby-pamby stuff for Kentucky: It's a criminal offense there to fire a gun that isn't loaded. Tough on crime, that's Kentucky! Can't you hear the police dispatcher call: "Car Fourteen, proceed to convenience store. Use extreme caution. Shots fired from unloaded gun."

Institutionalized racism: Oklahoma law says the only time a person may legally carry a gun is while being "chased by an Indian." I thought Indians were persons. And can Native Americans legally carry guns while being chased by non-Indians?

Fashion prejudice: Burdoville, Vermont requires all women who carry guns to avoid wearing high heels. Gun-toting women may have shoe heels no more than one and a half inches high.

But in Bourbon, Mississippi, only men and law officers can carry a wooden gun. Probably because women aren't dumb enough to carry a wooden gun.

Well, folks, that's Gun Law, U.S.A.

ZZZZZZ...

State Can't Stay Up

In Washington State the gun controllers have this little problem. Not only are they bunglers at controlling criminals, they also can't keep up with the paperwork they demand of gun owners.

In early 1995 a woman bought a 17-ounce model revolver because it was light enough to carry all day. She shelled out $379.95 for it. She also filled out the gun owner's form required by the state Department of Licensing to record her purchase.

They probably didn't record it for a year.

Despite a law that says the state should keep records of handgun buyers (for their up-to-date computer database) the paperwork for more than 70,000 handguns purchased at commercial gun stores the previous year sits in boxes at the Department of Licensing in Olympia.

They are a year behind. The flood of gun purchases resulted from the Brady Bill, which made people rush to buy guns before they became unavailable.

Three employees whose job it is to record those gun transactions have been inundated with other work, according to state officials.

Other work?

Wait a minute. If gun purchase registration was so important while it was being debated in the Legislature, why does "other work" now come first?

Here's the answer: Pat Brown, administrator in charge of the firearms section, says even though a name might not be entered on the computer, her employees can put their hands on the paperwork. Few law enforcement agencies actually request gun information, she said.

On the other hand, Steve Perry, a supervisor in the Edmonds, Washington, Police Department, said that when police seize a weapon and check its serial number, the state computer often yields nothing.

Well, well. Law abiding citizens who register their gun purchases don't use guns to commit crimes! And people who use guns to commit crimes use unregistered weapons! What a surprise!

So the expensive system that can't keep up with the paperwork backlog isn't very useful anyway. It seems to me we said that while the Legislature was debating the issue.

I have a better idea.

Maybe we should have a waiting period for gun control laws.

Two Out Of Three Doctors Think

The Rest Are For Gun Control

The Left keeps a careful watch on the Right in American politics. But it's careful to hide the fact that it's the Left.

Like The Violence Policy Center. It "researched" reports on violence. One was "Assault Weapons and Accessories in America," another was "Assault Weapons: Analysis, New Research and Legislation."

Gee, I wonder what their stand on gun owners might be?

This outfit used to be called the New Right Watch. They had trouble with that, because it doesn't take an Einstein to figure out that if you're watchdogging the Right, you're the Left.

So, the name underwent a little cosmetic surgery, and now the patient is looking much better. Much more credible. More acceptable to the unwitting public.

But the Left by any other name is still—

Well, the Left.

And the Violence Policy Center gets its money largely from Foundation grants—big money foundations protecting their own privilege and elite position.

Here are a few more national organizations with anti-gun policies:

AFL-CIO

American Academy of Child and Adolescent
    Psychiatry
American Academy of Pediatrics
American Alliance for Rights and Responsi
    bilities
American Association of Retired Persons
American Association of School Administra
    tors
American Association for the Surgery of
Trauma
American Bar Association
American Civil Liberties Union
American Medical Association
American Trauma Society
Coalition to Stop Gun Violence
Common Cause
Dehre Foundation
Handgun Control, Inc.
National Association of Community Health
    Centers
National Association of Police Organizations
National Association of School Psychologists
National Coalition Against Domestic Violence
National Education Association
National Safe Kids Campaign

Honest George

Would You Buy
A Used Gun From This Man?

Flashback: The Dan Quayle Memorial Gun
Control Chat, with apologies to Art Buchwald:
"Guns are so unsafe, Dan. We have to control them. Let's put air bags on them."
"But, George, tests show that air bags can
save a person only half the time. A 50 percent
vote is a stalemate. I see it in the Senate."
"What about seat belts, then, Dan? We could
attach one to the barrel of the gun and you'd have
to buckle up before the trigger would work."
"Well, George, two out of three sport shooters say it restricts them from firing at their target.
What about bumpers on pistols?"
"Good thinking, Dan. If a gun went off acci-
dentally, it might keep your hand from getting
smashed. But I think a real solution to the gun

safety problem is a collapsible pistol grip so that when the gun hits something, the grip automatically crumples."

"I don't know, George, I think we'd have that problem with hand injuries again. And our focus groups show that most bullet wounds are in the neck. How would we prevent whiplash?"

"Well, Dan, we could encourage people to wear bulletproof vests and drive low in their seats."

"A great idea, George. That would protect against driveby shootings on the freeway, too."

"That's it, then, Dan. We've hit on the perfect gun control solution. Air bags, seat belts, collapsible grips, and driver education. I think we should stump on that in the re-election campaign."

"Four more years, George."

"Two terms, Dan."

Crime Without Punishment

Only Gun Control is Politically Correct Criminal Control Isn't

The American people want to crack down on criminals.

But among the nation's elite, only gun control is acceptable.

That's the conclusion of John J. DiIulio, professor of politics and public affairs at Princeton University and a fellow in governmental studies at the Brookings Institution.

"Solid majorities of Americans, including overwhelming majorities of African-Americans, believe that criminals who assault, rape, rob, burglarize, deal drugs or murder should be arrested, prosecuted and punished in a swift and certain fashion," DeIulio told the *Wall Street Journal.*

Well, can you imagine the liberal media saying that?

DeIulio says what I have been saying for

years: That the American people "believe that violent and repeat criminals should be imprisoned; that a prison sentence of X years should mean a prison sentence of X years (truth-in-sentencing); that criminals with multiple convictions should receive long prison sentences or life without parole; and that capital punishment is warranted on both social and moral grounds."

But do the policy makers and the liberal elite listen? Not likely.

The sorts of people who have been cheering the Clinton administration's lack of criminal control keep talking down to us of the need to "educate the public" about the virtues of alternatives to incarceration. I'm educated.

DeIulio says that "Prison is now the alternative sentence: about three out of every four convicted criminals (more than three million people), are on the streets without meaningful probation or parole supervision.

"Only 42% of reported murders result in a prison sentence; most convicted murderers spend well under 10 years behind bars.

"The Swiss cheese of mandatory sentencing has left little room behind bars for petty, first-time or non-violent criminals. More than 93% of state prisoners are violent criminals (with two or more felony convictions) or violent repeat criminals. Most of the 'property offenders' behind bars have long criminal histories and a propensity for violence.

"Within three years about two-thirds of all probationers get into serious trouble with the law again, and 20% of released property offenders are rearrested for a violent crime.

"Today, only some 7% of burglaries in the U.S. ever result in an arrest, and barely 1.2% ever result in imprisonment."

What's the government spending on criminal control? "Barely half a cent of every government dollar (federal, state and local) goes to keeping convicted criminals behind bars, and just over three cents goes to all criminal justice activities (cops, courts and corrections)."

We really like that, don't we?

No, we don't!

The American people know what the Clinton administration doesn't: America has crime without punishment. If we are ever to restore confidence in government, that's got to stop.

DeIulio spoke for a lot of us when he said, "As years of pubic frustration with crime have begun to boil over, the people are being subjected to a last-ditch anti-incarceration dodge: Even though public spending on prisons relative to other government activities is a pittance, it would 'cost too much' (we are told) to imprison all violent repeat criminals for all or most of their terms; even if crime pays, stiffening sentences, abolishing parole and adding prisons won't help."

I hear that silliness all the time.

But you and I know the truth: Prison pays for most prisoners. It's costly to let crooks roam loose. They rob. They kill.

I recall that a 1987 Justice Department study analyzed the social costs and benefits of imprisonment. The liberal elite went ballistic. They don't want prison to have any social benefits.

But one of DeIulio's own studies showed that it costs about twice as much to let a criminal roam the streets as it does to keep him behind bars.

Prison is twice as beneficial as letting crooks go loose.

The people know that.

The government knows that.

Yet Bill Clinton wants to slice up the gun rights of law abiding citizens while doing nothing to control criminals—worse than nothing: making the world safe for criminals. No jail. Disarmed victims. Crooks love that setup.

So here we all sit, surrounded by crooks that our criminal justice system won't control, and Bill Clinton pushes a Gun Ban "Crime Bill" and the Brady Bill that make it impossible for us to defend ourselves.

Time to stop this nonsense.

Time for criminal control.

Gun control has had its shot, and it missed.

2001
A Clinton Odyssey

Here we are at the end of the book. As a fitting close, I give my final words to J. Richard Reynolds of Crown Point, Indiana. He wrote this marvellous mythical radio news broadcast from 2001.

"Turning now to crime: The quarterly crime statistics were released today and as expected, murder, robbery and rape have once again dramatically increased.

"Listeners will recall when President Bill Clinton was re-elected in 1996, he appointed the then Vice President Hillary Clinton, later elected president in 2000, as the chairperson of a special blue ribbon panel to review violent crimes. Bill Clinton, now the nation's First Gentleman, serves as personal secretary to Ms. President.

"Hillary Clinton and her panel successfully argued that 'honest, law-abiding citizens would not want to own a weapon of any kind. What are we anyway—barbarians?'

"The panel further argued that all home owners should be required to install security systems to prevent crimes in lieu of owning weapons.

"Those who do not have adequate security systems to stop crime will be guilty of inducing and inviting criminals to act in a manner in which otherwise they probably would not have. Once again, she urged the American people to be patient.

"Ms. President concluded by saying, 'Besides, having the death penalty and owning a handgun were never deterrents to crime. Just ask any criminal.'"

Think about that after you close this book!

Well, we're all done for now. Goodbye, dear reader. I've had fun. I hope you've had fun.

Oh, yes, I shouldn't forget after thinking about that mythical radio broadcast:

Say goodbye, Bill!

Bye, folks. And Alan, I'm really not anti-gun, so stop pickin' on me so much, would you please?

Now you can enjoy the Merril Press **Politically Correct** series of clever, tasteless, thought-provoking, hilarious and downright philosophical humor books. See the last page in this book for a special offer.

Politically Correct Hunting, written and illustrated by Ken Jacobson. Of course, there's no such thing as politically correct hunting, so Ken Jacobson takes a romp through the cherished beliefs of animals rights activists while sharing his many years of real outdoor experience as a hunter and guide.

Politically Correct Environment by Alan Gottlieb and Ron Arnold, with cartoons by Chuck Asay. Two leaders of the Wise Use movement poke a whole lot of fun at stuffy, self-righteous eco-pests, with political cartoons by one of America's boldest newspaper cartoonists.

Politically Correct Guns, by Alan Gottlieb. A take-no-prisoners sortie deep behind enemy lines among the gun control crowd, jabbing them with their own hypocrisy and stupid actions, written by a leader of the gun rights movement.

Mail to: Merril Press, PO Box 1682, Bellevue, WA 98009
Telephone orders: 206-454-7009   FAX orders: 206-451-3959

If you have enjoyed **Politically Correct Guns**, you'll want these other exciting titles from Merril Press.

Trashing the Economy: How Runaway Environmentalism is Wrecking America, by Ron Arnold and Alan Gottlieb, 670 pages, paperback, $19.95.

It Takes A Hero: The Grassroots Battle Against Environmental Oppression, by William Perry Pendley. 346 pages, paperback, $14.95.

Storm Over Rangelands: Private Rights in Federal Lands, by Wayne Hage, 288 pages, paperback, $14.95.

Stealing the National Parks: The Destruction of Concessions and Public Access, by Don Hummel, 428 pages, hardcover, $19.95.

Ecology Wars: Environmentalism As If People Mattered, by Ron Arnold, 182 pages, paperback, $14.95.

The Wise Use Agenda, edited by Alan Gottlieb, 168 pages, paperback, $9.95.

Mail to: Merril Press, PO Box 1682, Bellevue, WA 98009
Telephone orders: 206-454-7009 FAX orders: 206-451-3959

Just When You Thought It Was Safe To Go Back Into The Bookstore...

...You find there are more of these outrageously crazy **Politically Correct** books of clever, tasteless, thought-provoking, hilarious and downright philosophical humor. Each is 180 pages, three quality paperbacks for the price of two! $30.00 plus $2.00 each for shipping and handling...a total of $36.00 for a ton of fun.

Get all three
And be P.C.!

Politically Correct Hunting, written and illustrated by Ken Jacobson. Of course, there's no such thing as politically correct hunting, so Ken Jacobson takes a romp through the cherished beliefs of animals rights activists while sharing his many years of real outdoor experience as a hunter and guide.

Politically Correct Environment by Alan Gottlieb and Ron Arnold, with cartoons by Chuck Asay. Two leaders of the Wise Use movement poke a whole lot of fun at stuffy, self-righteous eco-pests, with political cartoons by one of America's boldest newspaper cartoonists.

Politically Correct Guns, by Alan Gottlieb. A take-no-prisoners sortie deep behind enemy lines among the gun control crowd, jabbing them with their own hypocrisy and stupid actions, written by a leader of the gun rights movement.

Use either of the order forms on the previous two pages for this special offer!

What They're Saying About Alan Gottlieb

"Gottlieb is a well known and recognized champion of gun rights."
—*Arms Collectors Journal*

"Every gun owner should read this book and get a good laugh at their opponents."
—*Gun Week*

"The pro-gun movement has a truly remarkable advocate in Alan Gottlieb."
—former U.S. Senator Steve Symms

"Eloquent voice sides with gun owners...it's not easy to dismiss Gottlieb, Chairman of the Citizens Committee for the Right to Keep and Bear Arms and founder of the Second Amendment Foundation."
—*Cleveland Plain Dealer*

"Gottlieb, author of what is described as the definitive book on the subject."
—*The Seattle Times*

"Alan Gottlieb's book The Rights of Gun Owners— a bible of the pro-gun movement."
—*The New Yorker*

"Alan Gottlieb has given us a wonderfully biting satire on the anti-gun crowd in his new book, Politically Correct Guns. Women need this book on their nightstands—next to their handgun."
—*Women and Guns Magazine*